Shift: The Playbook for Event-Driven Architecture Advocacy.

Fran Mendez

Shift: The Playbook for Event-Driven Architecture Advocacy.

ISBN: 978-84-09-76152-4

Ordering Information: Quantity sales. Special discounts are available on quantity purchases by corporations, associations, and others. For details, contact the publisher at https://leadtheshift.co.

Disclaimer

Educational Purposes Only. The information provided in this book is for educational and informational purposes only. While the author has made every effort to ensure the accuracy of the strategies and tactics presented, they are provided "as-is" without warranty of any kind.

No Professional Advice. The content of this book is not intended as a substitute for professional legal, financial, or technical advice. Readers are encouraged to consult with qualified professionals before implementing any significant business or technical changes described herein.

Results May Vary. The success of the strategies mentioned depends on various factors beyond the author's control, including market conditions, individual implementation, and existing infrastructure. The author and publisher do not guarantee specific outcomes or results from following the tactics in this book.

Liability. The author and publisher shall have neither liability nor responsibility to any person or entity with respect to any loss or damage caused, or alleged to have been caused, directly or indirectly, by the information contained in this book.

To Eva, my wife, my best friend, and the love of my life.
Thanks for always being there.

To Ada, my daughter, and the new love of my life.
Stay curious bichina.

Contents

Introduction

You know it in your gut. You've seen the tangled mess of point-to-point integrations, the brittle services that break every time a new feature is added, and the endless meetings trying to figure out why a simple change takes three months to deploy across five different teams. You see the solution clearly: a shift to an Event-Driven Architecture (EDA). An architecture built on asynchronous communication, where services are loosely-coupled, resilient, and can evolve independently. An architecture that moves as fast as the business needs it to.

You've done the research. You've read the technical books. You can talk about idempotent consumers, distributed transactions, and the CAP theorem until you're blue in the face. You've sketched out the designs on whiteboards, you've built a cool proof-of-concept, and you're ready to go.

And then you walk into a meeting with your manager, your director, or the budget committee. You start explaining the benefits of using a message broker like RabbitMQ or Google Cloud Pub/Sub. You talk about loose-coupling and scalability. And you see their eyes glaze over. They ask, "How does this help us hit our quarterly revenue target?" or "This sounds like a huge, risky science project. What we have works fine." Your brilliant technical solution, the one that you know will solve so many of the company's deep-seated problems, is a total non-starter.

You are here if you've ever felt that frustration. You're here if you know that technology is only half the battle. The other half—the harder half—is about people. It's about communication, influence, and strategy.

This is not another technical manual on how to implement EDA. There are plenty of great books for that. This book is different. This is your playbook for advocacy.

It's a guide to the human side of architectural change. It's about how to get your brilliant ideas out of your head, off the whiteboard, and into production. It's about how to convince your colleagues, your managers, and your company's leaders that shifting to an event-driven mindset isn't just a good technical decision, but an essential business strategy.

Over the years, building and evangelizing AsyncAPI, I've learned a hard lesson: the best specification and the best technology in the world are useless if you can't get people to understand, adopt, and champion them. I've seen incredibly smart engineers fail not because their ideas were bad, but because they couldn't build the coalition needed to make them a reality. Trust me, I have failed on many of these multiple times myself. I've also seen other teams succeed, not because they had more resources, but because they understood how to navigate the organization. This book is a collection of the strategies that work.

Why This Playbook Will Be Your Go-To Resource

I wrote this book to be the guide I wish I had. It's built on a simple premise: advocating for architectural change is a skill you can learn. It's not about being a slick salesperson or a master politician. It's about having a clear set of strategies—a playbook—that you can pull from when you face a specific challenge.

Instead of talking in vague hypotheticals, this book gives you concrete tactics. Each chapter is a self-contained strategy designed to overcome a specific hurdle you will face on your EDA journey. From getting that first 'yes' from a skeptical manager to managing the inevitable resistance from teams who are comfortable with the old way of doing things, this playbook has a move for you.

This is the bridge between your technical expertise and organizational impact. It will teach you how to translate complex architectural concepts into the language of business value, how to build allies, how to create momentum, and how to turn your vision into a company-wide reality.

Navigating Your Strategies: How to Use This Book for Maximum Impact

Think of this book less like a novel and more like a field manual. It's not designed to be read sequentially from cover to cover, though you certainly can. It's designed to be a reference you can jump into whenever you hit a roadblock.

The book is organized into a series of Strategies. Each one follows a consistent structure so you know exactly what to expect:

- The Scenario & The Challenge: We start by setting the scene with a relatable story and a clear "You are here if…" statement. This helps you immediately identify if the strategy is the right one for your current situation.
- The Core Principle: This is the single, powerful idea at the heart of the strategy. It's the mental model you need to adopt to solve the problem.
- The Action Plan: This is the core of each chapter. It's a set of 3-5 practical, step-by-step tactics you can implement immediately. These are your plays.
- Story Time: To show these strategies aren't just theory, each chapter includes a story from the trenches. These are real, anonymized accounts shared with me by EDA practitioners at various companies who were generous enough to let us learn from their successes and their scars.
- Common Pitfalls: I'll share some hard-won wisdom on what not to do. Avoiding these common mistakes can be just as important as implementing the right tactics.
- Key Takeaways: A scannable summary of the chapter's most critical, actionable advice. Think of it as your final checklist before you head into your next meeting.
- Further Reading: No strategy exists in a vacuum. Here, I'll point you to a curated list of books, articles, and resources that I've found genuinely useful for going deeper on the topic.

Is your leadership team ignoring your proposals? Jump to the strategy on securing executive sponsorship. Are you struggling to get other teams to adopt the new standards you're proposing? There's a strategy for that. Each one is a self-contained module designed for immediate, practical application.

The EDA Advocate's Mindset: Core Principles for Success

Before we dive into the specific plays, it's important to ground ourselves in a few core principles. Your mindset is the foundation upon which all these strategies are built. Without the right perspective, even the best tactics will fall flat.

- You're Selling Outcomes, Not Architecture. This is the most important shift you need to make. Nobody buys "Event-Driven Architecture." They buy what it enables: faster time-to-market, lower operational costs, improved customer experience, or the ability to innovate without breaking everything. Stop talking about Kafka streams and start talking about how you can eliminate shipping delays. Stop talking about loose-coupling and start talking about how product teams can launch features independently without waiting for a coordinated release. Always translate the technology into a business outcome.

- Resistance is Data. When a team or an individual pushes back on your idea, it's easy to get frustrated and label them as "dinosaurs" or "not getting it." This is a mistake. Resistance is not just an obstacle; it's a valuable signal. It's data. It tells you that you've missed something. Perhaps you haven't addressed a legitimate fear about operational complexity. Maybe their current system has a hidden benefit you don't understand. Or maybe they feel their expertise is being threatened. Your job is not to crush resistance but to understand it. Listen, ask questions, and use that data to strengthen your proposal.

- Progress Over Perfection. The dream of a "big bang" rewrite of your entire company's architecture is a fantasy. It's too big, too risky, and too expensive for any sane leader to approve. The successful advocate knows that change happens incrementally. Find one, small, painful problem and solve it with an event-driven approach. Build a "lighthouse" project that demonstrates tangible value. Show, don't just tell. A small, successful project is your most powerful tool for building momentum and earning the trust to take on bigger challenges.

- You Are a Translator. As an EDA advocate, you live in two worlds: the technical world of services, events, and brokers, and the business world of KPIs, ROI, and strategic objectives. Your most critical role is to be a translator between these two worlds. You must be able to explain the business implications of technical decisions to leaders and the strategic context of business goals to your fellow engineers. Mastering this translation is the key to unlocking influence.

This journey—this shift—is about more than just technology. It's a change in how your organization thinks, communicates, and builds. It's a challenge, no doubt. But it's a challenge you can win. This playbook will show you how.

Welcome to the **shift**.

Foundational Strategies

Setting the Stage for Success

Strategy 1

Discovering Strategic Value

Picture this: You walk into a high-stakes meeting with your VP of Engineering and the Chief Product Officer. You're buzzing with excitement. For weeks, you and your team have been whiteboarding a brilliant plan to re-architect your core services around an Event-Driven Architecture (EDA). You launch into your presentation, your slides filled with elegant diagrams of brokers, topics, and asynchronous flows. You talk about loose coupling, resilience, and scalability. You explain how this new architecture is technically superior in every way.

Ten minutes in, you look up from your laptop. The CPO is scrolling through emails on his phone. The VP is nodding politely, but her eyes have that distant, glazed-over look. When you finish, there's a short, awkward silence. The CPO looks up and asks, "So, how does this help us hit our quarterly revenue target?" You stammer, trying to connect the dots on the fly about long-term velocity. But it's too late. The meeting ends with a polite, "Thanks for the presentation, we'll consider it," which everyone in the room knows is corporate-speak for "no." You walk out defeated, your brilliant technical solution dead on arrival.

This mistake is incredibly common. It's a mistake you're probably at risk of making right now. You see a powerful technical solution, but you haven't built the business case for it. You're trying to sell the how before anyone has agreed on the why.

You are here if...

- Your brilliant proposals for long-term architectural improvements are consistently shot down with questions like, "What's the immediate ROI?" or "We don't have the budget for non-feature work."
- You feel like you're speaking a different language from your product, sales, or leadership teams. You talk about tech debt and scalability; they talk about user acquisition and market share.
- You see your organization drowning in technical problems—slow deployments, cascading failures, tangled systems—but you struggle to make anyone outside of engineering see the urgency.
- You're excited about the potential of EDA, but you don't know where to start building a coalition of support. You feel like you're on an island.

If any of this sounds familiar, you're in the right place. This isn't a technical problem; it's a communication and strategy problem.

Here's the single most important idea in this chapter, the one that will completely change your approach. Get this right, and everything else falls into place: Stop pitching Event-Driven Architecture. Start solving expensive business problems that EDA just so happens to fix.

Read that again. Your job is not to be the "EDA person." Your job is to be a business-problem solver. Leaders don't fund technical projects; they invest in business outcomes. They don't care about Kafka topics or RabbitMQ exchanges. They care about reducing customer churn, accelerating speed to market, cutting operational costs, and beating the competition. EDA is simply a powerful tool to achieve those goals. You must learn to frame your entire advocacy around the problems people already want to solve, not the solution you want to build.

The Action Plan

So how do you go from being a tech advocate to a business-problem solver? You have to do your homework. This means getting out of your code editor and becoming a detective inside your own organization. Your mission is to uncover the most significant, costly, and urgent pains that leadership would pay to make disappear.

Tactic 1: Become a Pain Detective

Your first move is to listen and learn. People love to talk about their problems, and you need to be the person they talk to. The goal here is to collect raw intelligence from the front lines.

- Start with your team: You and your engineering peers are already feeling the pain. Make a list. Does it take weeks to deploy a simple change? Are you constantly getting paged because of cascading failures? Do you spend more time untangling dependencies than writing new code? These are symptoms of deeper issues. They are your first clues.
- Talk to Customer Support (CS): The CS team is a goldmine. They are on the receiving end of every user frustration. Join their Slack channel, ask to shadow a call, or just grab coffee with a CS agent. Your opening line is simple: "What are the top three things our users complain about all the time?" Practice empathetic listening. Don't defend the system; don't explain why things are the way they are. Just listen. You'll start to hear patterns: "The product is slow," "Notifications never arrive," or "My data is out of sync between the mobile and web app." These are not just complaints; they are business problems. Write them down.
- Connect with Sales and Solution Engineers: These folks are on the front line of revenue. They know exactly why you lose deals. Ask them, "Have we ever lost a big customer because we were missing a key feature or couldn't integrate with their systems?" or "What are the biggest technical roadblocks to closing a seven-figure deal?" They might tell you about the inability to provide real-time data to a key prospect or the months it takes to implement a custom feature they need to sign. When a technical limitation directly costs the company money, leadership pays attention.
- Sit down with Product Managers: Product Managers live in the gap between what users want and what engineering can deliver. They feel the pain of slow development cycles more than anyone. Ask them: "What's the one feature you wish we could build but can't because our current system makes it too hard?" or "How much faster could we innovate if our services weren't so tightly coupled?" They'll tell you about the competitive pressures and the frustration of watching nimbler competitors ship features while you're stuck in bureaucratic gridlock.

Tactic 2: Decode the View from the Top

While front-line pain is powerful, you must also understand what keeps your leaders up at night. You need to connect your findings to their strategic priorities.

- Watch the All Hands meetings: This is the easiest way to learn what the C-suite cares about. Go back and watch the last three recordings. What are the recurring themes? Are they talking about expanding into a new market? Improving operational efficiency? Scaling the business? These are your strategic guideposts. Any problem you identify should ultimately tie back to one of these goals.

- Ask for 15 minutes: It sounds scary, but asking a director or VP for a brief chat can be incredibly insightful. Don't go in with a solution. Go in with honest curiosity. A great way to frame it is: "I'm trying to better understand the company's key challenges for this year so I can make sure my team is focused on what matters most. From your perspective, what are the biggest hurdles we need to overcome?" You're not bothering them; you're showing initiative and strategic thinking. Listen for words like "scalability," "adaptability," "market changes," and "competitive advantage."

Tactic 3: Map the Strategic Landscape

Once you've collected all these pain points, they can feel like a messy, disconnected pile of complaints. You need a way to organize them to see the bigger picture. This is where a powerful strategic tool called a Wardley Map is incredibly useful.

Think of a Wardley Map as a way to draw a map of your business landscape, just like a general would map a battlefield. Here's the simple idea:

- Start with the user need: At the very top, you place the user or customer and their need (e.g., "Share project updates with my team").

- Map the value chain: Below that, you map out all the components and activities needed to fulfill that need. This chain goes all the way from the user-facing parts of your app down to the underlying infrastructure like compute and storage.

- Plot its evolution: Here's the magic. You place these components on a horizontal axis based on how evolved they are—from Genesis (brand new, chaotic, high risk) on the left, to Custom-Built, to Product (like a SaaS tool you buy), and finally to Commodity (stable, boring, like electricity) on the right.

This map gives you a visual superpower. You'll immediately see where the bottlenecks and high-friction areas are. You might discover that a critical customer-facing feature (high up the chain) depends on a clunky, inefficient, custom-built system that is holding everything back. That spot on your map is a perfect target for an EDA-based solution. It's a visual "X marks the spot" that helps you move from "we have a bunch of problems" to "this is the precise, strategic intervention we need to make."

Tactic 4: Connect Pain to a Potential Cure

Now you have a list of raw business pains. Your next step is to start mapping them to the potential solutions that EDA offers. You're not architecting the whole system yet; you're just drawing a clear, straight line between a specific problem and a specific capability of EDA.

Let's say you discovered these pains:

- Pain: The sales team complains that by the time they get a lead from the marketing system, it's hours old and has gone cold.
- EDA Cure: An event-driven approach could publish a "New Lead" event the instant it's captured. The sales CRM could subscribe to this event and create a task for a salesperson in seconds, not hours.
- Pain: Customer Support is overwhelmed with calls about late shipments because the inventory system and the order system only sync up once a night.
- EDA Cure: With EDA, an "Order Placed" event could trigger immediate checks against a real-time inventory service. An "Item Shipped" event could instantly notify the customer. This moves the whole process from batch to real-time.
- Pain: The product team wants to launch a new recommendations feature, but it's impossible because user activity data, product data, and purchase history are locked in different monolithic databases.
- EDA Cure: Each service could publish events ("User Viewed Product," "Item Added to Cart," "Order Completed"). A new, separate recommendations service could simply subscribe to this stream of events to build its model, without ever needing to touch the original monoliths.

See the pattern? You're not saying, "We should use EDA." You're saying, "We have this specific problem, and here's a conceptual way we could solve it by having our systems talk to each other in real-time."

Tactic 5: Translate Tech Wins into Business Language

This is the most crucial translation you will ever make. You have to take your technical "cure" and describe its benefit in the language of business value. If you can't do this, your advocacy will fail. It's the lesson Maria from our opening story learned the hard way.

Here's a simple translation guide:

- Instead of: "Loosely coupled services and asynchronous communication."
- Say: "Faster time-to-market. We can have multiple teams work in parallel without breaking each other's work. This means we can launch that new partner integration in one month instead of three."
- Instead of: "Real-time event processing."
- Say: "A better customer experience that increases loyalty. We can instantly detect a potentially fraudulent transaction and text the customer, or notify them the second their package ships. Happy customers buy more."
- Instead of: "Enhanced system resilience and fault isolation."
- Say: "Reduced risk and lower costs from downtime. If our recommendations engine goes down, it won't crash the checkout process. This means we stop losing money during outages."
- Instead of: "Independent scalability of components."
- Say: "Lower infrastructure costs. During a flash sale, we can scale up just the order processing service instead of our entire massive monolith, saving a lot on our cloud bill."

Always ask yourself: Does this statement explain how we make money, save money, reduce risk, or beat the competition? If not, rephrase it until it does.

Tactic 6: Build a Preliminary Business Case

Talking about value is good. Putting numbers to it is what gets projects funded. You don't need a perfect, 50-page report at this stage, but you do need some back-of-the-napkin math to show this is a serious proposal. This is your first attempt at quantifying the Return on Investment (ROI).

- Estimate Cost Savings: Look at the pain points. If downtime costs the company $100,000 per hour and you have a major outage every quarter, reducing that by half is a $200,000 annual saving. If developers spend 20% of their time on bug fixes caused by system entanglement, how much is that in salary costs?

- Project Revenue Generation: Talk to Sales or Product. If faster leads could increase the conversion rate by just 2%, what does that mean in new revenue per year? If you can launch a new premium feature six months earlier than the competition, what's the projected revenue for those six months?

- Quantify Efficiency Gains: If you can automate a manual process that takes three people half their time, you've just freed up 60 hours of work per week. That time can now be spent on value-adding activities instead of administrative drag.

Be conservative with your numbers and be honest about your assumptions. The goal isn't to present a fake, perfect number. The goal is to show that you've thought through the financial impact and that the potential benefit is big enough to justify further investigation.

Story Time

This story has been contributed by David Roldán Martínez, AI Governance & Compliance Strategist.

> Every new banking partner used a different API. Different quirks. Different authentication. Different rate limits. For developers, each integration was like decoding an alien language with no Rosetta Stone. Weeks of custom adapters, endless testing, and sandboxes that lied about production behavior.
>
> Meanwhile, the sales team was stuck. Deals slowed to a crawl. Clients waited impatiently. Revenue opportunities slipped through the cracks. Everyone felt the pressure, like juggling flaming torches while riding a unicycle, with no safety net.
>
> When I first stepped into the client engagement, I quickly realized why their integration process was a nightmare…and it was only a matter of time before someone dropped the ball.
>
> That's when I realized there had to be a better way…and I flipped the script.

I found myself in a conference room with the client's Head of Architecture, Maya, and Head of Product, Ravi. The frustration in the room was palpable.

I opened my laptop, pulled up a diagram, and said:

Me: "I think I see a path out of this nightmare. What if we stop treating every bank API as a completely unique problem?"

Maya (skeptical): "We've tried that. Every bank is different: different authentication, different data structures, different rate limits. We've built adapters for months, and it still isn't fast enough."

Ravi (frustrated): "Clients are waiting. Every delay is lost revenue. We can't keep patching this with custom code."

I leaned in, drawing a simple flow on the whiteboard.

Me: "Instead of building full adapters for every API, we create a standardized API gateway. Every bank publishes events ('New Transaction,' 'Account Updated,' 'Balance Alert') in a format we define. Then, our internal apps, dashboards, and portals just subscribe to these events."

Maya: "So… we don't need to rewrite integrations for every system?"

Me: "Exactly. We only build lightweight connectors to map each bank's API to our common event schema. Once that's done, everything downstream gets updated automatically, in real time. It's event-driven architecture at its simplest: publish once, consume anywhere."

Ravi's eyes lit up.

Ravi: "So instead of weeks of manual coding for every new bank, this could cut onboarding to… what? Weeks?"

Me: "Or even days, once the first few connectors are in place. And the IT team stops fighting APIs and starts delivering real business value."

Maya leaned back, nodding slowly.

Maya: "It's ambitious. But if it works, it turns integration from a headache into a strategic advantage."

That conversation was the turning point. I proposed a standardized API gateway paired with an event-driven architecture (EDA) system.

The results were immediate and undeniable.

Integration timelines dropped from months to weeks.

Client onboarding accelerated. Revenue that might have been lost was preserved.

The IT team shifted from firefighting APIs to focusing on business value.

And leadership began to see integrations not as a slow, painful chore but as a strategic enabler.

Complexity doesn't have to slow you down. Standardization and event-driven design can turn chaos into opportunity. What once seemed like an impossible juggling act became a coordinated, reliable system, and a competitive advantage for the client.

From this experience, I learned a critical lesson: Sometimes, the best solution isn't writing more code. It's changing how the system thinks.

Common Pitfalls

As you put this strategy into action, watch out for these common traps. They're easy to fall into but just as easy to avoid if you see them coming.

- × Leading with the technology. Avoid starting any conversation with "We should use EDA" or "I think we need Kafka." You immediately put people on the defensive and frame the discussion around cost and complexity. Always lead with the business problem.
- × Treating estimates as facts. Your initial ROI calculations are educated guesses. Be clear about that. If you present them as hard numbers and someone pokes a hole in one of your assumptions, you lose credibility. Frame it as, "Based on these assumptions, we could potentially save…"
- × Solving problems nobody cares about. You might find a technically interesting problem that is super fun to solve, but if it doesn't align with a strategic priority for leadership or a major pain point for a key department, your project will go nowhere. Focus on the pain that has a budget attached to it.

Key Takeaways

- ☞ Strategic Discovery is Critical: Identify organizational pain points before proposing EDA solutions.

- ☞ Focus on Business Problems: Common issues include siloed systems, slow processes, scaling challenges, and delayed feature delivery.
- ☞ Connect Technical Solutions to Business Value: Translate EDA benefits into tangible outcomes like faster time-to-market, improved customer experience, and reduced operational costs.
- ☞ Quantify the Impact: Calculate potential ROI through cost savings, revenue generation, and efficiency gains.
- ☞ Speak Business Language: Frame technical benefits in terms of making/ saving money, reducing risk, improving customer satisfaction, and increasing competitive advantage.

Further Reading

To go deeper on this, I strongly recommend two resources that will help you master the art of framing your solution from a business perspective.

- 🕮 **Wardley Maps by Simon Wardley**: This is the source. The book is available for free online through the Creative Commons license. Reading it will give you a fundamental understanding of strategy and situational awareness. It's not a light read, but mastering this technique will change how you view every business and technical challenge.
- 🕮 **The Mom Test**: How to talk to customers & learn if your business is a good idea when everyone is lying to you by Rob Fitzpatrick: This book is essential for the "Pain Detective" tactic. It teaches you how to ask good questions that prevent people from just being polite and telling you what they think you want to hear. It will help you uncover their genuine problems, which is the raw material you need to build a compelling case.
- 🕮 **Value Proposition Canvas by Strategyzer**: This is a simple but incredibly powerful visual tool. It forces you to map your customer's (i.e., your organization's) pains and desired gains directly to the features of your proposed solution. It's the perfect one-page guide to ensure you're focused on what truly matters to the business.
- 🕮 **Good Strategy/Bad Strategy**: The Difference and Why It Matters by Richard P. Rumelt: This book is a masterclass in strategic thinking. It will teach you how to diagnose a business challenge, create a guiding policy, and design coherent actions. It will help you elevate your proposals from simple technical ideas to well-reasoned strategic initiatives.

Strategy 2

Mapping the Stakeholder Landscape

Imagine this. You've spent weeks, maybe months, putting together a brilliant proposal for shifting a core part of your company's system to an Event-Driven Architecture (EDA). You've got the diagrams, the performance projections, the tech choices dialed in. It's a work of art. You walk into the big meeting with the VP of Engineering and a few product leaders. You start your presentation, talking about brokers, asynchronous communication, and service decoupling. Five minutes in, you see it. The eyes glazing over. The subtle phone-checking under the table. When you finish, the first question isn't about scalability or resilience. It's, "So how many engineers does this take, and what features are we not shipping this quarter to do it?" Your brilliant technical solution just slammed into a wall of human reality. The best technology doesn't win on its own; it wins because the right people decide to back it.

Driving a change as big as EDA isn't just about writing good code; it's about navigating a complex web of people. Each person has their own goals, fears, and view of the world. Trying to push your vision without understanding this landscape is a recipe for frustration and failure. You're setting yourself up for a long, hard fight that you'll probably lose.

You are here if...

- You have a solid technical vision for EDA, but you feel like you're talking to a brick wall when you try to explain it to others.
- Your proposals are consistently shot down with questions about immediate Return on Investment (ROI) and budget, while the long-term strategic benefits you see so clearly are completely ignored.
- You see engineering teams nodding along in meetings but then going back to their desks and doing things the old way, quietly resisting the change.
- You feel like you're speaking a different language than the business leaders, product managers, and even other technical teams. You talk about decoupling, and they hear "delay." You talk about resilience, and they hear "risk."

Here's the fundamental idea that will change how you approach this: An architectural shift is a political campaign, not a science experiment. Your job is not just to be right about the technology; your job is to build a winning coalition of support. You win by understanding the motivations of the voters—your stakeholders—and crafting a message that resonates with what they truly care about. You have to stop thinking like a pure engineer and start thinking like a strategist. Your map to victory isn't a system diagram; it's a map of the people.

The Action Plan

To win this campaign, you need a playbook. This isn't about shady office politics; it's about professional empathy and smart communication. You need to systematically map the terrain, understand the players, and build the relationships that will turn your vision into a reality.

Tactic 1: Draw Your Map of the World

Before you can persuade anyone, you have to know who to talk to. Your first job is to identify every single person and group who has a stake in this change. You need to cast a wide net, because influence doesn't always follow the official org chart.

- Start with the Obvious: List the leaders. Your manager, the VP of Engineering, the Chief Technology Officer (CTO), the Chief Information Officer (CIO). These are the people who control budgets and give the final green light. But don't stop there. Include the heads of Infrastructure, Data, Security, and Platform Engineering. EDA will cross into their territory, and you need them in the conversation early.

- Follow the Workflow: Think about the entire lifecycle of a service.
- Engineering Teams: Who will actually build, test, and run these new event-driven services? Identify the tech leads and the senior engineers who hold a lot of sway. Their buy-in is everything. If they fight you, your project is dead on arrival.
- Product Managers: They decide what gets built. If they don't see how EDA helps them launch features faster or create better user experiences, they will never prioritize the work.
- Operations and Site Reliability Engineering (SRE): These are the people who get paged at 3 AM. They will have very strong and very valid opinions about how to monitor, deploy, and manage these new systems. Ignore them at your peril.
- Follow the Money and the Value: Who in the business benefits if this works? Think about departments like Sales, Marketing, Finance, or Logistics. Does EDA solve a data problem for them? Does it enable a new feature that will drive revenue? The leaders of these departments can become your most powerful non-technical allies.
- Find the Real Influencers: Every company has them. They might not have a fancy title, but they are the "go-to" people. They're the architects everyone respects or the senior engineers whose opinions carry more weight than a manager's. A great way to find them is to ask other developers, "If you're really stuck on a hard problem, who do you go to for advice?" Their endorsement can be a massive shortcut to winning over the broader team.

Your final step is to put this all down on paper or in a document. Create a simple stakeholder map. List the names, their roles, and their teams. This map is your guide. It's a living document that you will update continuously as you learn more.

Miro has a great guide to Stakeholder mapping: https://miro.com/blog/stakeholder-mapping/#h-what-is-stakeholder-mapping.

Tactic 2: Decode Their Motivations (and Fears)

Once you know who the players are, you need to figure out what drives them. This is the most critical part of the process. You have to move beyond titles and roles to understand the human being on the other side of the table. Your goal is to figure out their "WIIFM"—What's In It For Me?

For each person on your map, you need to have one-on-one conversations. Your goal in these chats isn't to sell; it's to listen. Ask open-ended questions: "What are the biggest challenges your team is facing right now?" "What are your main goals for this year?" "If you could wave a magic wand and fix one thing about our current systems, what would it be?"

As you listen, you're trying to uncover a few key things:

- Their Objectives: How is their success measured? What are their Key Performance Indicators (KPIs)? If you can connect EDA directly to helping them hit their goals, you've found a powerful angle.
- Their Motivations: Are they trying to climb the career ladder and want to be seen as an innovator? Are they a problem-solver who just wants to get rid of technical debt? Are they motivated by making their team's life easier?
- Their Influence: Do they have formal authority (they can approve budgets) or informal influence (people just respect their opinion)? Knowing this tells you how they can help you.

Most importantly, you need to become a "fear detective." Big architectural changes are scary. People don't resist change because they are difficult; they resist because they are afraid of something. It is your job to uncover these fears, validate them, and have a plan to address them. Pretending they don't exist is a fatal mistake. Listen for these common fears:

- Fear of the Unknown / Learning Curve: People worry if they can keep up. They fear their skills will become outdated or that they'll look incompetent. You'll hear this in questions like, "How much training are we going to get for this?" or "My team is already swamped; how are we supposed to learn all this?"
- Fear of Complexity: EDA can look like a chaotic spider web of services if it's not done well. Stakeholders worry about how they'll ever debug a problem that crosses ten different services. They'll talk about "too many moving parts" or "debugging nightmares."
- Fear of Cost: New infrastructure, new tools, and the time engineers spend learning all have a price tag. Business leaders will ask, "How much is this all going to cost?" and "What's the ROI?"
- Fear of Risk and Instability: The "if it ain't broke, don't fix it" mindset is powerful. People worry that you'll break the existing, stable systems during the migration. They'll ask about rollback plans and the impact on existing Service Level Agreements (SLAs).

- Fear of Vendor Lock-in: If you propose using a specific cloud provider's messaging service, people will rightly worry about being tied to that vendor forever, subject to their pricing and whims.

- Fear of Job Security: This is the fear that's rarely spoken aloud but is often the most powerful. Will this new architecture make my role or my team's skills irrelevant? This fear often hides behind what looks like irrational resistance.

When you hear these fears, don't argue. Acknowledge them. "That's a really valid point. The learning curve is a real concern, and we need a solid plan for it." By validating their fear, you build trust and turn an adversary into a collaborator.

Tactic 3: Sort Your Players into Roles

As you gather this information, you can start categorizing your stakeholders on your map. This helps you focus your energy where it will have the most impact.

- Champions: These are your true believers. They get it. They're excited about the possibilities and are willing to use their influence to help you. Your job with champions is to empower them. Give them information, talking points, and public praise. Make them your co-presenters.

- Allies: These people are open to the idea but might have some reservations. They are persuadable. Your job is to nurture them. Give them the information they need to address their specific concerns. Show them small wins from a pilot project. Your goal is to turn an ally into a champion.

- Neutrals: Most people will start here. They don't have a strong opinion yet because it's not on their radar. Your job is to educate them with clear, simple updates. Don't ignore them; their collective opinion can tip the scales.

- Blockers (or Skeptics): These are the people who are actively resistant. Your first instinct might be to fight them, but that's a mistake. Your job is to understand them. Their resistance almost always comes from one of the fears listed above or a legitimate concern you've overlooked. Listen deeply to their objections. They might be pointing out a huge flaw in your plan. You don't have to convert every blocker. Sometimes, the goal is just to neutralize their opposition by addressing their core concern, so they don't actively work against you.

Tactic 4: Speak Their Language

You wouldn't give the same speech to a group of investors and a group of software engineers. The final piece of the action plan is to tailor your message for each audience. Stop using a one-size-fits-all presentation.

- For Business Leaders (VPs, Finance, Product): No deep technical jargon. None. Frame everything in the language of business outcomes: reducing cost, increasing revenue, mitigating risk, or improving customer satisfaction. Use their metrics. Instead of saying, "We can decouple the checkout service," say, "We can reduce the risk of the entire site going down during a sales event, protecting our revenue."
- For Technical Teams (Engineers, Ops, SREs): Here, you can go deeper. Talk about the "how." Discuss architectural patterns, technology choices, and the developer experience. But be brutally honest about the challenges. Address their fears about debugging and operational complexity head-on. They will respect your transparency far more than sales hype. Show them how this makes their lives better, with better tools and fewer frustrating dependencies.
- For Blockers and Skeptics: Your communication here should start with listening. Use one-on-one meetings. Acknowledge their concerns. "I understand why you're worried about performance. Let's look at the latency numbers from the pilot." Provide data and evidence to address specific, fact-based concerns. For fear-based concerns, offer reassurance and concrete plans for training, support, and phased rollouts.

Have a look at the The "Shift" Communication Style Guide (check out the Resources section at the end of the book). This guide provides practical tips and examples on how to adjust your language, tone, and content for different types of stakeholders. It'll cover things like translating technical benefits into business value, framing arguments for skeptics, and providing the right level of detail for different audiences.

Story Time

I once learned this lesson the hard way. A friend and I were hired to build an internal platform to standardize how third-party integrations were built. The company had a huge problem: different teams were building the same integrations over and over, each with its own security flaws and bugs. It was a costly, inefficient mess.

Our platform was a technical masterpiece. It was secure, fast, and would save the company a fortune in duplicated work. We built three new integrations on it in two days during a conference, blowing away potential partners. We were promising engineering teams, "You just write the business logic; we'll handle all the annoying plumbing." It seemed like a total win.

But we made a critical mistake. We didn't map the entire stakeholder landscape. A large part of our European office was composed of engineers whose entire job was to maintain just two of the old, clunky integrations. Our platform, if successful, would eventually make their current work—and maybe even some of their roles—redundant.

What we didn't know was that the leadership in that office had a hidden goal: to grow their headcount and increase their influence in the global company. A project that threatened to reduce their team size was a direct threat to their political power. The day after I returned from my successful trip, our project was "frozen." It was dead. We had built amazing technology that solved a huge business problem, but it failed because it conflicted with the unstated, personal goals of a powerful group of stakeholders. That experience taught me forever: understanding the real motivations is not a nice-to-have; it's everything.

Common Pitfalls

As you put this strategy into practice, watch out for these common traps. They're easy to fall into.

- ✕ Mistaking silence for agreement. When you present your idea in a big meeting and no one objects, it's tempting to think everyone is on board. They're not. They are either processing, indifferent, or, worse, waiting to voice their objections privately to their teams. You have to follow up one-on-one.
- ✕ Treating blockers as enemies. It's easy to label someone who raises objections as "difficult" or "political." But more often than not, a skeptic is pointing to a real risk you've underestimated. Their concerns are valuable data. Listen to them, and you might just save your project from a huge mistake.
- ✕ Using a one-size-fits-all pitch. The same presentation deck will not work for your CTO, your product manager, and your senior engineers. Sending the same email to everyone is lazy and ineffective. If you don't tailor your message to what each audience cares about, you're not really communicating; you're just making noise.

Key Takeaways

- ☞ People First, Then Tech: Shifting to Event-Driven Architecture is as much about people as it is about technology. If you don't get the human element right, the best tech in the world won't save you. Understanding your stakeholders isn't optional; it's fundamental.

- ☞ Cast a Wide Net: When you're figuring out who your stakeholders are, think broadly. It's not just the execs. It's the engineers in the trenches, the product managers, the folks in various business units, and those quiet but super influential technical gurus.

- ☞ Dig Deep on Motivations and Fears: Don't just scratch the surface. You need to get what makes each stakeholder tick – their goals, what's in it for them (WIIFM), their real influence, and especially their fears. Concerns about the learning curve, complexity, cost, risk, and even job security are common and valid. Listen to them.

- ☞ Know Your Allies (and Your Blockers): Sorting stakeholders into Champions, Allies, Neutrals, and Blockers helps you focus your efforts. But remember, these aren't fixed labels. People can and do change their minds as they learn more.

- ☞ One Message Doesn't Fit All: Tailor your communication. Speak business language to business folks, get technical with tech folks. Understand their world and frame EDA in terms that matter to them**.

- ☞ Use Your Tools: That Stakeholder Map Template and Communication Style Guide aren't just for show. They are practical tools to keep you organized and effective. Use them, update them, make them your own.

Further Reading

To go deeper on the human dynamics of change and influence, these books are an excellent start. They aren't technical books, but they contain the wisdom you need to lead a technical transformation.

- 🕮 Getting to Yes by Roger Fisher and William Ury. This is the classic guide to negotiation, but its core principles are about understanding the interests behind people's positions—exactly what you need to do with stakeholders.

- 🕮 Immunity to Change by Robert Kegan and Lisa Lahey. This book provides a powerful framework for understanding why people (and organizations) so often resist changes that are in their own best interest. It's an advanced look at the hidden fears that drive behavior.

Strategy 3

Crafting a Compelling Narrative

You're in the big meeting. You've got your slides ready. They're packed with diagrams showing how your proposed Event-Driven Architecture (EDA) will decouple services, improve data flow, and increase system resilience. You talk about idempotent consumers, message brokers, and schema registries. You've laid out a technically perfect case. You finish, look up, and are met with... polite smiles and blank stares. An executive thanks you for the technical deep dive and asks, "This is interesting, but what does it mean for our Q4 revenue goals?" Your proposal is dead on arrival, not because it was wrong, but because you presented a blueprint when they needed to see a picture of the finished home. You had all the facts, but you didn't have a story.

You are here if...

- You have a rock-solid technical solution but can't seem to get anyone outside of your immediate team excited about it.
- Your proposals for architectural improvements are consistently shot down because they're seen as "just tech stuff" with no clear link to business outcomes.
- You know EDA can solve real problems, but you're struggling to translate the how (the technical details) into the so what (the business value).

- You feel like you're speaking a different language from the people whose support you absolutely need to make progress.

The core principle is this: People don't invest in technical specifications; they invest in compelling stories that solve their problems and promise a better future. Facts and figures are supporting characters, but the story is the hero. Your job as an advocate is not just to be an architect of systems, but to be an architect of understanding. You must build a narrative that connects the technical capabilities of EDA directly to the business and operational pains your organization feels every single day. A good story makes the abstract feel concrete, the complex feel simple, and the future feel achievable.

The Action Plan

To move from a dry technical pitch to a compelling narrative, you need a plan. It's not about being a novelist; it's about being a strategic communicator. Here are the tactics to build a story that gets people on board.

Tactic 1: Define Your Core Message

Before you write a single slide or open your mouth, you need to know the one thing you want your audience to remember. This is the heart of your story, the hook for everything else. A weak core message is forgettable; a strong one sticks.

Your core message must be:

- Simple and Clear: Use plain business talk. No jargon. If you can't explain it to someone in marketing in 30 seconds, it's too complicated.
- Focused on Value: What is the single biggest win? Does it cut development time in half? Does it eliminate the outages that frustrate customers? Does it unlock a feature everyone wants?
- Specific to Your Company: Generic benefits like "improved scalability" are meaningless. Connect it to your organization's actual headaches.

Let's look at the difference. A bad core message sounds like: "We should adopt EDA to enable asynchronous, decoupled microservices for improved scalability and resilience." It's technically accurate but puts everyone to sleep.

A good core message sounds like:

- "We can cut our new feature launch time from six months to six weeks by letting our systems react to business events in real time."
- "We can finally stop the system-wide outages caused by a single service failing, making our platform dramatically more reliable for our customers."

To find your core message, force yourself to answer these questions:

- What is the single most expensive or frustrating problem that EDA solves for us?
- What is the most exciting business opportunity this new architecture unlocks?
- If I got in an elevator with the CEO and had 30 seconds, what would I say to get them excited about this?

Nail this message first. Write it down. Make it the title of your proposal. It's your north star for every conversation that follows.

Tactic 2: Structure Your Story for Impact

Once you have your core message, you need a structure to deliver it. A jumble of facts, even good ones, won't work. You need to take your audience on a journey that's logical and persuasive. There are two incredibly powerful frameworks for this: one is perfect for tactical, problem-focused situations, and the other is built for inspiring a bigger, strategic vision.

Framework A: The Problem-Solution-Benefit-Call to Action (P-S-B-CTA)

This is your workhorse framework. It's direct, practical, and incredibly effective for most situations, from team meetings to project proposals.

- The Problem (The Villain): Start with a pain point that everyone in the room recognizes and hates. Make it tangible. Don't just say "integrations are hard." Say, "Remember last quarter when the new promotion feature was delayed by a month because we couldn't get the inventory and billing systems to sync up? That's the kind of headache that's slowing us all down." Use real examples of lost time, frustrated developers, or unhappy customers.
- The Solution (The Hero): Introduce EDA as the hero that slays this villain.

Explain the concept simply. "What if, instead of those systems being tightly wired together, they could just announce important things that happen? The inventory system could shout, 'Hey, 100 widgets just sold!' and any other system that cares, like billing or shipping, could just listen and react. That's the basic idea behind EDA."

- The Benefits (The Happy Ending): Paint the picture of the better world this solution creates. Connect the benefits directly back to the problem you started with. "By doing this, we're not just making things technically cleaner. We're talking about a future where a promotion feature can be built and launched in two weeks because the integration is no longer a bottleneck. We're talking about the billing system continuing to run even if the inventory system has a hiccup."

- The Call to Action (The Next Step): End with a clear, low-risk next step. You're not asking them to boil the ocean. You're asking them to take a single step with you. "So, let's prove this out. I propose we take the customer notification system, one of our biggest integration headaches, and build a small pilot using this event-driven approach over the next sprint. We'll learn a ton and have concrete data to decide where to go next."

Framework B: The Golden Circle (Why-How-What)

Popularized by Simon Sinek, this framework is for when you need to do more than just solve a problem; you need to inspire a movement. Use this when you're talking to leadership about a major strategic shift or trying to change the culture of your engineering organization.

- Start with WHY (The Purpose): This isn't about technology. It's about your organization's purpose or belief. "We believe that to win in our market, our teams must have the freedom to innovate at the speed of ideas, not at the speed of our clunky legacy integrations. Our core mission is to deliver value to customers instantly and reliably."

- Explain HOW (The Approach): This is your strategy for achieving that "Why." "We'll achieve this by changing the way our systems communicate. We're shifting to a model where information flows as real-time events, allowing our services to be independent, resilient, and yet seamlessly aware of each other."

- Detail WHAT (The Implementation): Finally, you get to the "What." "And what this looks like in practice is the adoption of Event-Driven Architecture. We'll use tools like Apache Kafka and define clear event contracts, starting with the new Customer Loyalty platform to lead the way."

P-S-B-CTA is for convincing the head with logic. The Golden Circle is for capturing the heart with vision. A smart advocate knows when to use which tool.

Tactic 3: Make the Abstract Concrete with Analogies

Terms like "asynchronous" and "decoupling" are huge turn-offs for non-technical audiences. Analogies are your secret weapon for making these concepts click. The goal is to connect a complex idea to something they already understand perfectly.

Here are a few you can steal and adapt:

- For Events: Think of them like news alerts on your phone. You subscribe to topics you care about. When something happens, a notification is pushed to you. You don't have to keep refreshing a website. This explains the real-time, push-based nature of EDA.
- For Decoupling: Use the restaurant kitchen analogy. The grilling station, salad station, and drink station all work independently. The grill chef just needs the order ticket; they don't need to know how the salad is made. If the drink machine breaks, the grill keeps running. This is how independent services in an EDA work, providing resilience.
- For Asynchronous Communication: Contrast a phone call with an email. A phone call is synchronous; both people must be available at the same time. It's blocking. An email is asynchronous. You send it, and the other person responds when they are ready. You can move on to other tasks. This perfectly illustrates the non-blocking nature of event-driven interactions.
- For the Event Broker: Think of it as a post office mail sorting center. You (the producer) drop off a letter at the post office. The post office (the broker) sorts it and guarantees it gets to the right mailbox (the consumer), even if they aren't home. It's the reliable delivery middleman.

When using analogies, keep them simple and don't stretch them too far. Their job is to create a quick "aha!" moment, not to be a perfect one-to-one map.

Tactic 4: Tailor the Narrative for Each Audience

A single story will not work for everyone. The CEO cares about different things than a junior developer. You must adjust your language, your examples, and the benefits you highlight for who is in the room.

- For Executives (CEO, CFO): Speak their language: risk, cost, speed, and competitive advantage. Focus on business outcomes. Frame EDA as a way to "cut time-to-market by 40%" or "reduce the risk of costly system-wide outages." Your call to action is for strategic approval and funding. Use the Golden Circle to paint a big, inspiring vision.

- For Technical Leaders (CTO, Architects): They bridge the gap between business and tech. Talk about architectural soundness, scalability, developer productivity, and maintainability. You can be more technical, but connect it to strategic goals. Highlight benefits like "true service decoupling" and "improving fault tolerance," which they know leads to better business outcomes.

- For Engineering Teams (Developers): They live in the code. Your story needs to answer "How does this make my job better?" Focus on how EDA reduces tedious boilerplate code, simplifies service logic, and allows them to work more autonomously. Show them diagrams. Give them code snippets. Your call to action is for them to try it, to learn it, and to help build it.

- For Product Managers: They care about customer value and feature velocity. Frame your narrative around what EDA enables for the product. "With this, we can finally build the real-time order tracking our customers have been demanding," or "We can get instant analytics on feature usage instead of waiting for a nightly batch job." Show them how EDA makes the product better, faster.

Always ask yourself: "What's in it for them?" Frame your story as the solution to their specific problems and the key to their specific goals.

Story Time

This is a story contributed by Emmanuel Paraskakis, Product Consultant for SaaS and API Companies with 15+ years in APIs.

> Our story takes place 13 years ago, at the infancy of APIs.
>
> I had just moved across the country after finding some initial success with an API product, was full of myself, and ready to rock!
>
> My new employer, a respected fintech, was relaunching its moneymaking legacy app as a SaaS platform, and I, as a brand new Director of Platform PM, knew precisely what they needed: An extensive API that lets users do everything programmatically.

But I was the only one in the company who saw it that way!

"Our UI is so flexible, well-designed, and easy to use that no one will ever need customization or integration - we don't need an API"

"Why build APIs when we have SQL - doh!"

"It's just developers, why would they need a well-designed API and good documentation?"

The Lead engineer was having none of it, and execs had no idea what APIs are.

My fate was decided: dream up specs for Auth, RBAC, and a Data Catalog, which, of course, were needed, but not differentiators.

But something kept telling me that this platform would benefit significantly from a good API, and the front end needed an organized way to get data.

I decided to do three things:

I would reach out to our design partners and global customers to see what they think. They were invested in our success, and if they didn't need APIs, well then so be it.

I would start an internal propaganda program to educate everyone about API-First, API Design, good docs, and all the goodness that comes with that.

I would learn everything I could about Data modeling, good API design, and testing so we could ship APIs with high quality, but also so that our hardcore engineers would trust me.

I started on No. 1, and to my surprise, our design partners, these Very Large Global Financial Corporations, were bought entirely in on having a full, usable, high-quality API for the new platform. They explained that for most workflows, they'd be embedding our back-end models into their process and that they cared about getting data in and out of our platform in an orderly way. The chief architect came on board, participated in these customer meetings with me, and saw the business benefits first-hand.

For No. 2, I started doing internal lunch and learns (brownbags) and would write a lot about APIs and how to do them right. I became known as "that API guy" and even put a distinctive plate on my car, "APIDUDE," so that people would see it coming in and out of the building - yes, in those days we would commute to an office! The CEO was now on board and spoke about APIs at the user conference keynote, as he understood that this was something customers demanded.

For No. 3, I started looking for information online and came upon the APICraft mailing list. Soon after, I went to the APICraft conference in Detroit and met all my future API friends. That got me on a path of learning and understanding the state of the art. I wrote my first API Standards doc and discovered API Blueprint and Runscope soon after.

We ended up building a large, high-quality (for the day) API platform, and I kept pushing the edge of complexity - this led me to start building API design tools, but that's another story!

Bottom-line: Customers and users are your allies. Your pure technical pitch is "just like your opinion, man".

Only when you express what you want to build in terms of benefits to the customer will you get the green light and find success!

Common Pitfalls

- × Avoid the One-Size-Fits-All Pitch: Presenting the same deep-technical slides to your CEO that you showed your engineering team is a guaranteed way to fail. Always adapt.
- × Avoid Overstretching Your Analogies: An analogy is a tool to explain one key point. If you try to make the restaurant kitchen map perfectly to every aspect of a message broker, you'll just confuse people and lose credibility. Make your point and move on.
- × Avoid Forgetting the Call to Action: A great story that ends with "...so, that's EDA" leaves the audience thinking, "Okay, and?" Always end with a clear, specific, and reasonable request. Tell them exactly what you want them to do next.

Key Takeaways

- ☞ Stories Sell, Not Just Specs: Facts are important, but a compelling narrative is what truly persuades people to embrace change like moving to EDA.

- ☞ Nail Your Core Message: Define a clear, simple, and value-focused reason for EDA adoption that's specific to your organization's pain points and goals.
- ☞ Choose Your Structure Wisely: Use P-S-B-CTA for direct, problem-solving narratives. Use the Golden Circle (Why-How-What) to inspire and connect to a larger vision.
- ☞ Analogies Make it Click: Use relatable analogies (like the restaurant kitchen or news alerts) to explain complex EDA concepts in an accessible way. Don't let jargon be a barrier.
- ☞ One Size Doesn't Fit All: Tailor your language, examples, chosen framework, and the benefits you highlight to resonate with diverse audiences – executives, technical leaders, engineers, and product managers. Speak their language.
- ☞ Make it Actionable: Always end your narrative with a clear call to action. What do you want your audience to do next?

Further Reading

- 🕮 For mastering the "Why-first" approach: Start with Why by Simon Sinek. It's the definitive guide to the Golden Circle and building inspiring narratives.
- 🕮 For structuring persuasive arguments: Made to Stick: Why Some Ideas Survive and Others Die by Chip Heath and Dan Heath. This book is a masterclass in making your ideas clear, memorable, and effective.
- 🕮 For understanding the human side of change: Immunity to Change by Robert Kegan and Lisa Laskow Lahey. It will give you a deeper appreciation for why people resist even logical changes, helping you craft more empathetic stories.

Persuasion Strategies

Winning Hearts, Minds, and Budgets

Strategy 4

Engaging the Engineering Team

Imagine you're in a team-wide meeting. You've just finished presenting your vision for moving to an Event-Driven Architecture (EDA). You've shown the beautiful diagrams, the clean separation of concerns, the potential for massive scale. You click to your final slide, feeling pretty good about it, and ask for questions.

And you get… silence.

A few people nod politely. One engineer in the back, a senior who has seen three different architectural paradigms come and go, has their arms crossed, a skeptical look on their face. Someone asks a polite but surface-level question about which message broker you'll use. The energy in the room is completely flat. There's no excitement, no curiosity, no buzz. You've laid out a technically sound future, but nobody looks like they actually want to go build it. It feels less like a call to adventure and more like another homework assignment.

You are here if…

- You have a technically solid plan for EDA, but you're struggling to get the very people who will build it excited. You find that:
- Your presentations on architectural theory are met with polite indifference.

- Engineers see the shift to EDA not as an opportunity, but as a mandate that means more work, new things to learn, and a disruption to their current, comfortable workflow.
- The benefits you talk about—like "decoupling" and "resilience"—sound like abstract management-speak and don't connect with the actual headaches developers face every day.
- You feel like you're trying to sell a blueprint, but your team just wants to know what tools they'll get to use and if it will make their jobs easier or harder.
- You know you can't force this change. For EDA to succeed, you don't just need compliance from your engineering team; you need their enthusiastic participation. You need them to want to build it this way.

The core principle is this: Engineers don't adopt architectures; they adopt better ways of working. Show them how EDA makes their job better, not just different.

Forget about selling the grand architectural vision from an ivory tower. Your job is to connect EDA to the day-to-day reality of a developer. The success of your advocacy hinges on your ability to answer the engineer's unspoken question: "What's in it for me?" They care about their craft, their autonomy, their tools, and their ability to ship cool stuff without a lot of friction. If you can frame EDA as a direct upgrade to their professional lives, you will transform skeptics into champions. It's not about the boxes and arrows on a diagram; it's about the feeling of empowerment when you get to own your service, the satisfaction of using modern tools, and the pride of building things that are fast and reliable.

While this strategy focuses on building excitement and highlighting the positive aspects of EDA, change can also bring up valid fears and concerns about complexity, testing, and debugging. It's crucial to address these head-on with honesty and clear solutions. For a deep dive into that, turn to Strategy 5: Addressing Developer Concerns.

The Action Plan

To turn your engineering team into a force of adoption, you need a proactive, hands-on engagement plan. This isn't about a single presentation; it's about creating a sustained campaign of education, empowerment, and two-way communication.

Tactic 1: Translate Architecture into Developer Joy

Before you even schedule your first brown bag, you need to reframe the benefits of EDA away from high-level architectural jargon and into the language of developer experience. Your engineers are on the front lines. They feel the pain of the current system most acutely. Speak to that.

- From "Decoupling" to "Autonomy": Don't just say services will be "decoupled." Explain what that actually means for them. "This means your team gets to own its service, end-to-end. You choose when to deploy, you control your own database, and you don't have to wait for three other teams to merge their changes before you can release your feature. No more giant, scary monolith deployments on a Friday." Autonomy is one of the most powerful motivators for a developer.
- From "Scalability" to "Modern Skills": Let's be honest, many developers are excited by technology. Frame the move to EDA as a chance to get hands-on experience with the tools that the most innovative companies in the world are using. Talk about learning Kafka, RabbitMQ, or Google Cloud Pub/Sub. Talk about building applications with modern frameworks designed for asynchronous communication. This isn't just a project; it's a resume-builder and a chance to stay relevant in a fast-moving industry.
- From "Resilience" to "Fewer Late-Night Pager Alerts": A tightly-coupled system means one service failure can cascade and bring the whole thing down. That's what gets people paged at 3 AM. Explain EDA's model of fault isolation. "When we build with events, the orders service going down doesn't have to crash the shipping notification service. The system can gracefully handle failures, queue up work, and recover. That means more robust systems and a more predictable on-call rotation for you."
- From "Extensibility" to "Easier to Add Cool Features": When you have an event stream, anyone can tap into it to build something new without touching the core service. Frame this as an innovation engine. "Imagine if the marketing team wants to run a flash sale analysis. Instead of you having to add custom logic to the checkout service, they can just build a new, tiny service that listens to OrderPlaced events. You don't have to change a thing. It makes saying 'yes' to new ideas way easier."

Tactic 2: Make It Tangible with Hands-On Learning

Engineers learn by doing. Slides are fine for context, but code is what builds conviction. Your goal is to get EDA off the whiteboard and onto their local machines as quickly as possible.

- The Killer Demo: A good demo is worth a thousand slides. But a great demo isn't a tour of a perfect, finished application. A great demo solves a real, relatable problem in real-time. Pick a common pain point in your current system—like a slow, complex reporting query or a process that requires polling three different APIs. Then, build a small, event-driven solution live (or with pre-scripted steps) that solves it elegantly. Show them the code. Show them the events flowing through the broker. Let them see how simple and powerful it can be.

- The Brown Bag Lunch: Brown bags are perfect for informal, focused education. Don't try to teach all of EDA in one session. Dedicate each one to a specific concept. One week, it's "What is an event and why is it different from a command?" The next, it's "A 15-minute intro to AWS EventBridge." Keep them short, practical, and leave a lot of time for Q&A. Bring in food. It makes it a social event, not a mandatory meeting.

- The Hands-On Workshop: This is your most powerful tool. The goal of a workshop is to have every single participant leave having successfully built a tiny event-driven system. Give them a GitHub repository with starter code and a clear README. Guide them through building a simple producer and a consumer that do something tangible, like processing a UserSignedUp event to send a welcome email. The feeling of "I built that, and it worked" is what creates real buy-in. Provide a virtual environment (like Gitpod or GitHub Codespaces) to eliminate the "it doesn't work on my machine" headache.

Tactic 3: Build a Communication Hub, Not a One-Way Street

Engagement is a two-way process. If you're just broadcasting information, you're doing it wrong. You need to create safe, accessible channels for engineers to ask questions, voice concerns, and share their own ideas.

- Create a Dedicated Channel: Set up a public Slack or Microsoft Teams channel named something like #ask-eda or #event-architecture. This becomes the central nervous system for your initiative. Post your slides, share interesting articles, and announce upcoming demos. Most importantly, make it the go-to place for questions.

- Establish "Office Hours": Set aside one or two hours a week where you (and other advocates) are available on a video call for anyone to drop in with questions. This is incredibly valuable for tackling complex problems that are too clunky for a chat message. It also shows that you are genuinely there to help, not just to dictate.

- Embrace All Questions: In your new channel and during office hours, you must foster psychological safety. Explicitly state, "There are no dumb questions." When someone asks something basic, thank them for asking because it's likely ten other people had the same question but were afraid to ask. If someone asks a skeptical or challenging question, thank them for their critical thinking. How you handle these early interactions sets the tone for the entire initiative. If you are defensive, you kill trust. If you are open and helpful, you build it.

Tactic 4: Find and Empower Your Champions

In any group of engineers, there will be a few who are naturally curious and excited by new technology. These are your future champions. Your job is to find them, nurture them, and give them a platform.

- Identify Early Adopters: They are the ones who ask insightful questions after your demo, who tinker with the sample code on their own time, or who post interesting articles in the chat.
- Give Them Early Access and Support: Invite this small group to a private channel or a "pioneer program." Give them early access to your tooling, your proof-of-concept (PoC) environments, and, most importantly, your time. Help them build something real. Their first-hand success will be your most powerful marketing tool.
- Pass the Microphone: Once an early adopter has successfully built something, ask them to present it at the next brown bag. A success story told by a peer is ten times more credible than one told by an architect or manager. It shifts the dynamic from "Here is what the architecture team wants" to "Look at this cool thing our colleague built, and here's how they did it." This creates social proof and makes adoption feel like a grassroots movement, not a top-down directive.

Story Time

I recently had a chat with a platform lead at a large global insurance company. He was facing a classic challenge. His team was building the foundation for a modern event-driven future but they were running into a wall of skepticism. The company's engineers were comfortable and productive with synchronous, request-response APIs. To them, EDA felt complex, immature, and filled with unknowns, especially around debugging and handling errors.

Instead of trying to enforce a top-down mandate from an architectural ivory tower, the platform team flipped the script. They stopped pushing EDA and decided to let the engineering teams pull for a solution.

Their strategy was simple but incredibly effective: they waited for teams to come to them with problems rooted in the synchronous world. A team would show up saying, "We have to keep polling this API every 30 seconds, and it's super inefficient," or "This chain of service calls keeps timing out and causing failures."

This was their opening.

Instead of offering a patch or a workaround, they would frame EDA as the direct answer to that specific headache. "The reason you're having this problem is because you're using a synchronous pattern for an asynchronous process," they'd explain. "If you publish an event instead, you won't have these issues." They weren't selling an architecture; they were solving a developer's immediate pain.

To lower the barrier to entry, they focused on two key things:

Empowering Champions: They identified motivated engineers in different teams who were willing to try the new approach. They worked closely with them, helped them succeed, and then let those engineers spread the word to their peers. A success story from someone on the front lines was far more powerful than any presentation from the platform team.

Providing Freedom within a Framework: They resisted the urge to dictate a single, rigid standard from day one. They understood that the EDA ecosystem was still maturing and that developers needed to experiment. So, they allowed teams to explore different protocols and patterns, treating them as internal customers whose feedback was essential. Their goal was to listen to the experiences of many teams and then, collaboratively, narrow down the choices to build a "paved road" that developers actually wanted to drive on.

The result was that adoption started happening organically. Engineers didn't feel like a new, complex architecture was being forced on them. Instead, they felt they were actively choosing a better way to work because it made their lives easier and solved their most frustrating problems.

Now, let's be clear: this wasn't a quick win. This journey took them years of patient work. It's only now, after letting teams explore and learn, that they are beginning to standardize on specific tools and patterns to manage complexity. And the most important part? They're doing it the same way they started: by collaborating directly with their internal customers, ensuring the new standards are a reflection of what the teams themselves have proven to work best.

Common Pitfalls

- × Avoid: The "Architecture Astronaut" Presentation. Do not fill your slides with dozens of abstract boxes and lines. Engineers are pragmatic. If they can't see how it connects to actual code and solves a real problem, you'll lose them. Always anchor your theory in tangible code and outcomes.
- × Avoid: The One-Off Demo. Don't do a single "big bang" demo and expect everyone to be converted. Engagement is a campaign. Use a steady drumbeat of demos, workshops, and office hours to keep the momentum going and reinforce the message. Take it easy, it's going to take months (sometimes more than a year) to get people aboard. Don't burn all your energy in a few weeks.
- × Avoid: Ignoring the "Why." Don't just show them how to use the new tools; constantly remind them why it's better. Connect every technical detail back to a developer-centric benefit like more autonomy, less on-call pain, or faster delivery.
- × Avoid: Canceling Office Hours Because "No One Shows Up." It's easy to get discouraged when you block out an hour on your calendar and no one joins for a few weeks straight. The temptation to cancel the meeting and reclaim your time is huge. Resist it. An empty office hours session isn't a sign of failure; it's a signal of consistency. The value is not just in the questions you answer, but in the psychological safety you create by being reliably available. Showing up to an empty meeting is a small price to pay to ensure that when an engineer finally does have a critical problem, they know exactly where to go and don't have to suffer in silence. Your consistency builds trust long before it fills a calendar slot.

Key Takeaways

- ☞ Empathy First: Connect EDA directly to solving their daily headaches and improving their work.
- ☞ Honesty Builds Bridges: Be open about challenges. Engineers respect realism. (Strategy 5 will arm you for detailed discussions).
- ☞ Show, Don't Just Tell (Repeatedly!): Demos, workshops, and pilot projects make EDA tangible and build skills.
- ☞ DevEx is King, Queen, and the Whole Court: Smooth tooling and clear processes are non-negotiable for adoption.
- ☞ Champions & Leaders are Your Multipliers: Empower peer advocates and get engineering leadership actively involved.

☞ Listen Actively & Be Receptive: Create an environment where engineers feel safe to voice concerns and ask questions.

Further Reading

- Team Topologies by Matthew Skelton and Manuel Pais: This book is essential for understanding how to structure your teams for autonomy and fast flow, which is a core promise of EDA. It provides the organizational blueprint for your technical one.

- Accelerate: The Science of Lean Software and DevOps by Nicole Forsgren, Jez Humble, and Gene Kim: This book provides the data to back up why things like decoupled architecture and empowered teams lead to higher performance. Use its findings to add weight to your arguments.

- The Business of Belonging by David Spinks: While focused on community building, its principles are directly applicable here. You are building an internal community of practice around EDA. This book will give you a playbook for how to foster that community, empower champions, and create a sense of shared ownership.

Strategy 5
Addressing Developer Concerns

Imagine this. You're in a room with your engineering team, the ones who live and breathe code every day. You've just finished presenting your vision for a new service, built on a shiny Event-Driven Architecture (EDA). You're excited. You talk about decoupling, resilience, and scalability. For a moment, the team seems to be with you, nodding along.

Then, the first hand goes up. "How do we debug this if a message gets lost between services?" Then another. "What does this mean for our on-call rotation? It feels like there are way more moving parts to break." And another. "This eventual consistency thing sounds like a recipe for weird data bugs. How do we test for that?"

Suddenly, the energy in the room has shifted. The initial curiosity has been replaced by a wave of anxiety. You see the skepticism on their faces. These aren't lazy developers trying to avoid work. These are the people who will be paged at 3 a.m. when something goes wrong. You realize you haven't just proposed a new architecture; you've proposed a new world of potential headaches and late-night emergencies they'll have to handle.

You are here if...

- You've laid out a plan to adopt EDA, and the most resistance is coming from the very people you need to build it. Their feedback isn't abstract; it's a list of very specific, practical worries.
- Your engineers are pushing back with statements like, "This is too complex," "It's going to slow down development," or, "This will be a total nightmare to operate and debug." You feel like you're trying to sell a powerful new engine, but all they can think about is how hard it will be to change the oil. You know the long-term benefits are huge, but their short-term fears are drowning out the message.

When developers push back, it's rarely because they're lazy or resistant to change for its own sake. They are pragmatists who are paid to anticipate failure. Their resistance is a rational response to perceived risk. They are the ones on the front lines, and they're doing their job by stress-testing your idea before a single line of code is written. Ignoring their concerns is not only disrespectful; it's a direct path to a failed project.

The core principle is: To win developers over, you must address their legitimate fears not with authority, but with empathy, evidence, and enablement. You have to stop selling and start solving. Your job is to make the new path feel less risky and more rewarding than the familiar one they walk today.

The Action Plan

To turn developer skepticism into genuine buy-in, you need a plan that goes beyond presentations. You need to get your hands dirty and solve their problems proactively.

Tactic 1: Acknowledge and Validate Fears Proactively

Don't wait for the tough questions to come up in a team meeting where you might be put on the spot. Address the elephant in the room from the very beginning. This shows that you've thought through the hard parts and respect their concerns.

The best way to do this is to create what I call a "Fear & Mitigation FAQ." This is a living document that you share before you even ask for feedback. In it, you explicitly list the most common developer fears about EDA and address each one head-on.

Your FAQ should include sections like:

Fear	Mitigation
Debugging is a nightmare in distributed systems.	You're right, it can be. That's why we are making distributed tracing a mandatory, day-one feature of our platform. Every event will carry a correlation ID, and our new observability tool will give you a single view of an entire workflow across multiple services. We'll show you exactly how it works before you start.
There's a steep learning curve.	Yes, there are new concepts to learn. We've allocated our next sprint for focused learning. We'll run hands-on workshops, provide access to curated online courses, and establish a pairing program where you can work alongside an experienced advocate.
Eventual consistency will cause endless data integrity bugs.	This is a real risk if not handled properly. Our approach is to use event-driven patterns only where business processes allow for it. For processes that require immediate consistency, we will continue to use synchronous patterns. We will provide clear architectural guidance and design patterns, like the Outbox Pattern, to ensure messages are sent reliably and idempotency is handled correctly in consumers.
The operational overhead will be huge.	More services can mean more overhead. That's why we're investing heavily in automation. Our platform team is building tools to automate the provisioning of topics, queues, and monitoring dashboards. Your team won't need to become Kafka or RabbitMQ experts; you'll use a simple CLI or a Git-based workflow to manage your resources.

By front-loading this information, you transform the conversation. You're no longer defending an idea; you're presenting a well-thought-out plan that anticipates and solves their biggest worries. More importantly, by sharing it and seeking (not just asking) for feedback, you're signalling that you're empathetic and take people's concerns seriously. It builds incredible trust.

Tactic 2: Make Learning Painless and Practical

Theory is boring. Nobody wants to read a 50-page whitepaper on event-driven theory before they can fix a bug. To get adoption, learning has to be hands-on, practical, and immediately applicable to a developer's daily work.

Run a Dojo or Hack Day: Set aside a day or two for a hands-on coding workshop. The goal isn't to build a production-ready system but to create a safe space to experiment. Give them a fun, low-stakes problem to solve, like building a real-time "like" counter for an internal blog or a notification system for CI/CD builds. Provide a working starting point and let them play. The goal is to build muscle memory and confidence.

Create a "Starter Kit" Repository: This is probably the single most effective thing you can do. Build a template repository for a new event-driven service. This isn't just a "Hello, World." It should be a production-ready skeleton that includes:

- A sample event producer and consumer.
- Connection logic for your message broker.
- Proper configuration management (no hardcoded secrets!).
- A full CI/CD pipeline that builds, tests, and deploys the service.
- Pre-configured observability: structured logging, metrics dashboards, and distributed tracing hooks.

With this starter kit, a developer can go from "idea" to "running service with world-class observability" in a matter of hours, not weeks. You've just lowered the barrier to entry to almost zero.

Record Short, Practical Videos: Create a library of 5-10 minute screen-capture videos that answer specific "how-to" questions. "How to Publish Your First Event," "How to Test an Event Consumer," "How to Find a Trace for a Failed Request." These are far more valuable than dense documentation for someone who is stuck on a specific problem.

Tactic 3: Provide a Rock-Solid "Paved Road"

Developers, like all of us, follow the path of least resistance. If doing things the "new way" is 10x harder than the "old way," they will find clever workarounds to stick with what they know. Your job is to make the new, correct path the absolute easiest path. This is often called building a "Paved Road."

- Abstract Away the Boilerplate: Create and support internal libraries that handle the messy parts of interacting with your event streaming platform. Your library should take care of serialization/deserialization, connecting to the broker, handling authentication, and implementing retry logic with exponential backoff. A developer shouldn't have to think about any of that. Their experience should be as simple as eventbus.publish(my_event) or @ eventbus.subscribe(topic).

- Automate Infrastructure with Self-Service: A developer should never have to file a ticket and wait two weeks for a new topic or queue to be created. This kills momentum. Implement an Infrastructure as Code (IaC) workflow using tools like Terraform or Crossplane. Let developers define their resource needs in a simple configuration file within their service's repository. When they merge a pull request, a pipeline automatically provisions the necessary infrastructure. This empowers teams and makes the platform team a true enabler, not a gatekeeper.

- Build Observability In, Not On: Don't just give teams a logging tool and a metrics dashboard and wish them luck. Integrate observability directly into your Paved Road. Your starter kits and libraries should come pre-instrumented. When a developer uses your tools, their service should automatically emit critical metrics (e.g., message throughput, consumer lag, processing latency, error rates) and generate traces for every event. They get best-in-class visibility for free, just by using your platform.

Tactic 4: Showcase "Local" Success and Build Internal Champions

A case study from Netflix or Uber is cool, but it's abstract. A success story from the team that sits on the next floor is real and incredibly persuasive. Peer-to-peer influence is your most powerful tool for driving adoption.

- Start with a Pilot Team: Don't try to boil the ocean and migrate everyone at once. Identify a single, friendly team that is working on a problem well-suited for EDA. It should be a system that is important but not so mission-critical that failure would be catastrophic. This will be your pilot project.

- Give Them "White-Glove" Support: Treat this pilot team like your most important customer. Give them everything they need to succeed: extra support, dedicated office hours, and your best engineers to help them over any hurdles. Their success is your success.

- Turn Them into Advocates: Once the pilot project is live and stable, you have your first internal success story. Now, market it. Ask the team's tech lead or a senior engineer to present their work at an all-hands engineering meeting or a brown-bag lunch session. Let them tell the story in their own words. Encourage them to be honest about the challenges they faced and how they solved them. This is far more credible than you, the advocate, presenting the same information.

- Celebrate and Amplify: Publicly celebrate the pilot team's win. Write about it in the internal engineering blog. Mention it in company newsletters. This creates powerful social proof. Other teams will see the success and think, "If they can do it, so can we." This is how you create a pull for your new architecture, instead of constantly having to push it on people.

Story Time

I was recently on a call with the leadership team of a major retailer. This wasn't a small company; they were a household name with thousands of employees, and they were pouring millions into a massive technological modernization. They had the right vision: break down their monoliths, move to microservices, and build a real-time enterprise with Apache Kafka at its core. On paper, they were doing everything right.

But the reality was a total mess.

They described a situation that was causing them immense frustration. They had built this beautiful, powerful "river" of real-time data with Kafka, meant to let every part of the business react instantly to things like sales, inventory changes, and customer actions. The problem? Their engineering teams were refusing to get in the water.

Instead of tapping into the real-time streams and processing events as they happened, teams were doing everything in their power to avoid it. They would connect to a Kafka topic, bulk-download all the data, dump it straight into their own private database, and then run their old, familiar overnight batch jobs against that stale copy. They had turned a high-performance streaming platform into the world's most over-engineered and expensive FTP server.

The company's dream of a unified "Golden Record" of data was dead on arrival. Instead, they had dozens of what one executive bitterly called "réplicas caca"—crappy replicas—all over the organization, each one slightly different and slightly out of date. They had all the operational complexity and cost of running Kafka, combined with all the data inconsistency and lag of their old batch world. It was the worst of both worlds.

The leadership team saw this as a clear-cut case of insubordination. But here's the funny part—if it weren't so tragic for their project. When the engineering teams asked the perfectly reasonable question, "Why should we use Kafka for this? Why are these new patterns better than what we have now?" the leadership couldn't actually give them a compelling answer.

They hadn't done the work to articulate why a real-time approach was better for a specific team's context. They couldn't explain the business value. Instead of acknowledging that some use cases might not be a good fit, or preparing solid arguments for the ones that were, they fell back on the only tool they had left: soft authority. Because they couldn't answer the "why," their message in meeting after meeting became, "You will adopt real-time patterns because this is our new company-wide direction."

This was a disaster. It signaled to the teams that the initiative wasn't a well-reasoned strategy but a top-down mandate without a solid rationale. What they got in return was not compliance. They got huge resistance, especially from the most senior engineers—the very people who had been at the company the longest and understood the business logic better than anyone. The more leadership pushed, the harder the teams resisted. The multi-million dollar investment was on the verge of complete failure, not because the technology was wrong, but because the human element had been completely ignored.

This story is the perfect illustration of what happens when you try to mandate change without addressing fear or even providing a good reason. The teams weren't replicating data because they were stubborn; they were doing it because it felt safer, and nobody had given them a convincing argument for why they should take on the risk of a new approach. They hadn't been given the tools, the training, or the psychological safety to feel confident in this new reality.

The path forward for this company wasn't a new dashboard or a stricter mandate. It was to stop talking and start listening. It was to go to the teams—without judgment—and explore the fears and legitimate questions that were driving this behavior. Their problem wasn't technical. It was a failure of leadership and empathy.

Common Pitfalls

As you implement this strategy, watch out for these common mistakes that can undermine your efforts.

- ✕ Avoid: Hand-waving away real concerns. Nothing kills trust faster than saying, "Don't worry about it, we'll figure it out later." If you don't have an answer to a tough question, the right response is, "That's an excellent point. I don't have a good answer right now, but I will investigate and come back to you with a concrete plan."
- ✕ Avoid: Providing tools without support. Just creating a "Paved Road" isn't

enough. You have to staff it. You need clear documentation, working examples, and a dedicated support channel (like a Slack channel or office hours) where developers can get help from a human being when they get stuck. A platform without support is just another piece of shelfware.

× Avoid: Focusing only on the "happy path." Developers spend most of their time thinking about what happens when things go wrong. When you demonstrate your new patterns, don't just show the successful workflow. Intentionally break things. Show them exactly what a failed message looks like in the dead-letter queue. Demonstrate how the retry logic works. Walk them through a distributed trace of a failed request. Showing them you have a robust plan for failure is more convincing than any happy-path demo.

Key Takeaways

☞ Developer skepticism is normal and valid. Your job is to engage with their concerns directly, not dismiss them.

☞ Don't guess their fears. Proactively listen to uncover their specific worries about complexity, testing, operational load, and the impact on their personal skills.

☞ Answer concerns with concrete solutions, not vague promises. Name specific tools like AsyncAPI, EventCatalog, and Microcks, and have a clear plan for infrastructure and support.

☞ A working internal prototype is the most powerful argument you have. If that's not possible, use highly relevant case studies to show that these problems are solvable.

☞ You can't win over everyone. Focus your energy on the willing and the curious. Build a coalition with your supporters rather than burning out on detractors.

Further Reading

🕮 Team Topologies by Matthew Skelton and Manuel Pais. This book is essential for understanding how to structure your teams and build the kind of platform that enables, rather than blocks, developer productivity.

🕮 The Fearless Organization by Amy C. Edmondson. A fantastic read on creating the psychological safety required for teams to feel comfortable experimenting with new, potentially scary technologies.

🕮 The AsyncAPI Documentation and Blog. For hands-on tutorials, best practices, and practical examples of documenting and working with event-driven systems. Our resources are designed to help you and your team get up to speed quickly.

Strategy 6

Securing Leadership Backing

You've been there. You're in the big conference room—the one with the expensive chairs and the fancy coffee machine. You've just spent twenty minutes walking the Chief Technology Officer and the Head of Product through a presentation you poured your heart into. It's a brilliant plan to re-architect a core part of your system around events. You've laid out the technical elegance, the decoupling, the improved data flow. You've shown diagrams of services communicating beautifully through a message broker.

You finish, feeling pretty good. You look up, expecting nods of approval, maybe even some excitement. Instead, you're met with polite but vacant stares. The CTO leans back, steeples their fingers, and asks the question that makes your stomach drop: "I see the technical diagrams, but what's the ROI on this? We have feature targets for this quarter. How does this help us meet them?"

The Head of Product chimes in, "And how long will this take? My team can't be blocked for six months on an infrastructure project."

Your brilliant technical proposal, the one that would solve so many downstream problems, just hit a brick wall. It feels like you were speaking a different language. And in a way, you were. You were talking tech to people who think in spreadsheets, risk assessments, and market share. Your project isn't dead, but it's definitely on life support.

You are here if...

- Your perfectly sound technical proposals are constantly getting shot down for not having a clear, immediate business impact.
- You struggle to answer questions about ROI, budget, and resource allocation from senior leadership.
- You know that moving to an EDA would solve a mountain of problems, but you can't seem to make the people holding the purse strings see it.
- You feel like an architect trying to convince a homeowner to replace the crumbling foundation of their house. You can see the cracks and know the long-term danger, but they're more interested in picking out new paint colors for the living room because that's the improvement they can see and show off right away.
- Your challenge isn't a technical one; it's a translation one. You need to learn to speak the language of business.

Here's the fundamental truth you need to internalize: Leaders don't fund technical projects; they invest in business outcomes.

Read that again. They aren't giving you money to implement Kafka or to decouple your services. They are giving you money to make the business more money, lose less money, or move faster than the competition. Your job as an advocate is to stop selling the how (the technical implementation) and start selling the why (the business value). Every single technical benefit of EDA—scalability, resilience, decoupling, data availability—has a direct counterpart in the language of business. Your task is to build that bridge, clearly and convincingly. You must translate your technical solution into the currency they trade in: dollars, risk, and time.

The Action Plan

Selling a vision requires more than just a good idea; it requires a strategy. You need to do your homework, build a rock-solid case, and present it in a way that grabs their attention and answers their questions before they even ask them.

Tactic 1: Become a Business Detective

Before you even start building your slide deck, you need to do some reconnaissance. You can't align your proposal with business priorities if you don't know what they are. Your goal here is to understand the company's strategic objectives from the perspective of the C-suite.

- Read the Official Documents: Get your hands on the latest annual report or quarterly earnings report. These documents are literally the company's promises to its investors. Look for keywords. Are they talking about "expanding into new markets," "improving operational efficiency," "reducing customer churn," or "enhancing security and compliance"? These are your golden nuggets. Your EDA proposal must directly support one or more of these goals.

- Listen to the Leaders: Pay close attention during company all-hands meetings. What are the CEO, CTO, and CPO talking about? What questions are they answering? What keeps them up at night? If the CEO is constantly talking about the threat from a new, nimble competitor, then "increasing development velocity" becomes a very powerful argument for your project.

- Talk to Your Business Counterparts: Go for coffee with product managers, marketing leads, or finance analysts. Ask them what their biggest headaches are. You might discover that the marketing team can't run effective campaigns because they don't have real-time customer data—a problem EDA is perfectly suited to solve. These conversations give you ground-level truth and potential allies.

Once you have this information, you can frame your entire pitch around it. You're no longer the tech person with a pet project; you're a strategic partner offering a solution to one of the company's most important problems.

Tactic 2: Build an Ironclad Business Case

Now that you know what leadership cares about, you need to build a document that explicitly connects EDA to those priorities. A vague promise of "things will be better" won't cut it. You need to quantify the value. Your business case should stand on three pillars: Money, Risk, and Speed.

Pillar 1: The Financial Argument (ROI)

This is about how your project will either make money or save money. Be as specific as possible.

- Cost Savings: Estimate the tangible savings. Will EDA reduce infrastructure costs by allowing for more efficient scaling? Will it lower operational overhead by reducing the number of outages and manual interventions? Calculate the cost of an hour of downtime for your critical systems and estimate how EDA would reduce that. For example: "Our current payment system experiences an average of 2 hours of downtime per quarter, costing us an estimated $250,000 in lost revenue annually. An event-driven redesign will increase resilience and is projected to reduce this downtime by 90%, saving $225,000 per year."

- Revenue Generation: How can EDA help bring in more money? The most common answer is faster time-to-market for new features. Work with a product manager to estimate this. "Our competitor launched a personalization feature 6 months before we could because our monolithic architecture slowed us down. If we can launch new features 30% faster with an event-driven approach, we can capture an additional $500,000 in market share over the next year."

Pillar 2: The Risk Mitigation Argument

Executives are paid to manage risk. Show them how EDA makes the business safer and more resilient.

- Operational Risk: The classic example is avoiding a single point of failure. A monolithic system going down can take the whole business with it. An event-driven system is more resilient; if one service fails, the others can often continue to operate. Frame this around business continuity. "Our current architecture means that a failure in the inventory system also brings down our checkout process, a huge risk during peak shopping seasons like Black Friday."

- Compliance & Security Risk: Events provide an immutable audit log of everything that happens in your system. This is incredibly valuable for compliance (like GDPR or SOX) and for security forensics. You can frame it as: "An event-driven approach gives us a complete, time-ordered log of all customer data changes, making audits simpler and reducing our risk of compliance fines."

Pillar 3: The Strategic Argument (Speed & Competitive Advantage)

This is about positioning the company to win in the future.

- Agility: This is the heart of the matter. EDA allows teams to work more independently. They can deploy their services on their own schedule without getting tangled up in the release cycles of other teams. This is a massive strategic advantage. Translate this into business terms: "By decoupling our teams, we can experiment with new product ideas in parallel, allowing us to respond to market changes faster than our monolithic competitors."

- Data as an Asset: EDA unlocks your data. Instead of being trapped in application-specific databases, business events are now available for any team to consume. This enables new capabilities like real-time analytics, machine learning models, and business intelligence dashboards that were previously impossible. "By making customer behavior events available in real time, the marketing team can trigger personalized offers instantly, increasing conversion rates, and the data science team can build a more accurate fraud detection model."

Tactic 3: Master the Executive Pitch

You've done your homework and built your case. Now you have to deliver it. When you walk into that room, you must project confidence and speak their language.

- Lead with the Problem, Not the Solution: Don't start with a slide titled "Event-Driven Architecture." Start with a slide that has a title like "Reducing Customer Churn by 15%" or "Accelerating Our Product Roadmap." State the business problem you're solving and its impact, using the data you gathered in Tactic 1.
- Structure is Everything: A good structure for a short executive pitch is:
- The Problem: Here is the business pain we are experiencing (e.g., "We are losing customers because our platform is unstable during peak loads.").
- The Impact: Here is what it's costing us in money, risk, or market position (e.g., "This cost us an estimated $1.2M last year and damages our brand reputation.").
- The Opportunity (Your Solution): We propose an architectural shift to solve this. Briefly name it ("a move to an event-driven model") but immediately pivot back to the benefits ("which will allow our systems to scale independently and handle 10x our current traffic.").
- The Ask: Here is the investment we need in terms of people and money (e.g., "We need a dedicated team of 4 engineers for 6 months and a budget of $50,000 for new tooling.").
- The Return: Here is the expected business outcome (e.g., "We project this will eliminate major outages, saving over $1M annually and protecting our brand.").
- Use Analogies, Not Jargon: You understand what an "idempotent consumer" is. They don't. And they don't care. Instead of using technical jargon, use a simple analogy. Compare a monolith to a restaurant where every single order, from drinks to dessert, has to go through one overworked chef. Compare EDA to a modern kitchen with specialized stations (a drink station, a grill station, a dessert station) that can all work in parallel, getting food out much faster and more reliably. It's a simple image, but it works.

Tactic 4: Pre-Socialize and Build Alliances

Never let the formal presentation be the first time an executive hears your idea. A surprise pitch is an easy pitch to reject. Your idea needs to have supporters in the room before you even begin.

- Find Your Business Ally: Identify a leader in a non-technical department (like Product, Marketing, or Sales) who is directly feeling the pain that your proposal solves. Work with them. Help them understand how your technical solution solves their business problem. When you finally present to the CTO, you can say, "Sarah from Marketing is on board with this, as it will give her team the real-time data they need for their new personalization campaign." Even better, have Sarah in the room with you, or have her co-present. An endorsement from a business peer is ten times more powerful than you arguing alone.
- One-on-One Previews: Schedule short, informal one-on-one meetings with the key decision-makers and influencers before the main meeting. Use this time to give them a preview of your idea and, more importantly, to listen to their initial reactions and concerns. This allows you to tailor your final presentation to address their specific objections head-on. It also makes them feel included in the process, turning potential critics into collaborators.

Story Time

The following is a story from David Pardo, experienced CEO, Investor, and Advisor.

When Fran reached out to me to ask for a real-world example of this chapter's issues, I had in mind a particular anecdote. After reading his first version of the text, I realized my experience was almost the same as what he had written about.

It was 2013. There were only a few EDAs, and we didn't even know that name yet. We had been working for a bit more than a year with a large retail company, and they had a problem. Their solution for purchase returns was slow, fragile, and expensive. It was a batch system that used a fork of commercial software relying on old tech to populate a database. Every time a customer came into one of the stores to return a purchase, there was a significant risk that the system wouldn't find the original invoice, and with a few million purchases daily, that opened the door to fraud, missing inventory and -above all- bad customer experience.

The key here was our business ally, Miguel. We had been working with him for a few years, and he had enough trust in our work that we could make a compelling case together. Don't forget that in a company everybody has to justify their decisions to somebody else.

We had the privilege of taking a year to develop the solution. We had to come up with things that a few years later would be patterns, standards, or even products, but didn't exist yet, like version-aware schema registries, real-time stream processing, or schema validation - all while using only the tech supported by the vendors.

Miguel had to put his job on the line more than once during that year. The pressure from the C-level people was immense, but it was one of those few occasions when rewriting it all made sense, since we had to replace the existing system with a whole different technology and a new paradigm.

In the end, everything worked. Twelve years later, it's still managing all PoS (Point of Sale) data at a rate of a few million sales every day - and you've probably used it without ever knowing any of this.

We promised a few things and luckily were able to overdeliver on all of them:

Faster responses: when we started, a purchase return query initially took a few seconds. After the migration, between 40 and 80 ms. That enabled us to use a single cluster for the whole world instead of one per continent.

Ability to reprocess messages: sometimes there were fiscal changes that had to be taken into account. We could modify and reprocess any event from the last quarter while keeping all historical data.

Complex rules: I didn't know there were so many rules governing returns. In some countries you're not allowed to return to a mall store something you bought on the high street.

If I had to choose a rule from Fran's list, it would be to build alliances. During a project those relationships will be strained, and you'll need to reassure them that everything is OK while using the same language. If you don't have that support yet, it's better to wait until you can find your business ally before starting with the rest of the sale.

Common Pitfalls

Even with a great plan, it's easy to stumble. Watch out for these common mistakes.

- × Avoiding the "Cost of Inaction." Sometimes, the most powerful argument isn't how great the future will be, but how painful the present is. Don't just sell the benefits of your proposal; sell the cost of not doing it. Quantify the pain of staying with the current system. "If we don't do this, we project that our system outages will increase by 50% next year as we scale, and we will not be able to launch the planned international expansion."
- × Proposing a "Big Bang" Revolution. Don't walk in and ask for a two-year, $5 million budget to rebuild the entire company from scratch. That's terrifying for any leader. Instead, frame your proposal as an incremental evolution. Propose a small, well-defined pilot project with a clear goal. "Let's start by re-architecting just the order confirmation service. It will take one team three months, and it will prove the value of this approach." A small, successful pilot builds trust and momentum, making it much easier to get funding for the next phase.
- × Getting Defensive During Q&A. When leaders push back with tough questions about cost, risk, or timing, they aren't necessarily attacking you. They are doing their job. Don't get defensive or technical. See their questions as a request for more information in their language. If they ask about risk, talk about your mitigation plan and the pilot project. If they ask about cost, refer back to your ROI calculations. Treat objections as an opportunity to reinforce your business case, not to win a technical debate.

Key Takeaways

- ☞ Leaders Fund Outcomes, Not Technology: This is the most critical mindset shift. Stop trying to sell Event-Driven Architecture. Instead, sell what EDA achieves: reduced operational costs, faster feature delivery, lower business risk, or the ability to enter new markets. Your entire approach must be built on this foundation.
- ☞ Align with Existing Strategy, Don't Invent a New One: Before you build your pitch, become a detective. Read the company's annual report and listen to all-hands meetings. Your proposal must directly connect to the stated strategic goals of the company—whether it's improving efficiency, reducing churn, or accelerating growth. Frame your project as an essential tool to help leaders achieve their goals.

- ☞ Build Your Case on the Three Pillars: Money, Risk, and Speed: A vague promise of "improvement" is useless. Your business case must be concrete and stand on three legs:
- ☞ Money: How will this project make or save the company money? (e.g., "Reduce outage costs by $500k/year").
- ☞ Risk: How will this make the business safer? (e.g., "Eliminate our single point of failure before the holiday shopping peak").
- ☞ Speed: How will this make the company faster and more competitive? (e.g., "Enable teams to launch new features 30% faster").
- ☞ Lead with the Pain, Not the Plumbing: Structure your presentation around the business problem. Start with the pain point and its quantifiable impact ("Our slow data processing is costing us customers."). Then, introduce your solution as the remedy. Use simple, powerful analogies (like the restaurant kitchen) to explain the concept, not deep technical jargon.
- ☞ Build Your Coalition Before You Present: Never let the big presentation be the first time stakeholders hear your idea. Socialize it one-on-one beforehand. Most importantly, find an ally in a business unit (like Product or Marketing) who feels the pain your project solves. A proposal championed by both Technology and Business is exponentially more likely to succeed.
- ☞ Propose a Pilot, Not a Revolution: Asking for a massive, multi-year budget to rebuild everything is a recipe for rejection. It's too big, too risky, and too slow. Instead, propose a small, well-defined pilot project with a clear, measurable outcome. A successful pilot builds incredible trust and momentum, making it much easier to secure funding for subsequent phases.
- ☞ Make Inaction Feel Expensive and Risky: Don't just focus on the benefits of your proposal; you must also clearly articulate the Cost of Inaction. What is the specific, quantifiable pain of staying on the current path? Show them that standing still isn't free—it's actively costing the company money, exposing it to risk, and allowing competitors to get ahead. This creates the urgency needed for them to act.

Further Reading

- 🕮 For mastering strategic thinking and framing: Good Strategy/Bad Strategy: The Difference and Why It Matters by Richard P. Rumelt. This book is essential for learning how to identify a core challenge and create a coherent action plan to overcome it.

- For linking technical work to business value: The Phoenix Project: A Novel About IT, DevOps, and Helping Your Business Win by Gene Kim, Kevin Behr, and George Spafford. It's a novel, but it's the best illustration out there of how IT work directly impacts business success.
- For navigating high-stakes conversations: Crucial Conversations: Tools for Talking When Stakes Are High by Kerry Patterson, Joseph Grenny, Ron McMillan, and Al Switzler. This book provides a fantastic framework for handling the tough questions and objections you'll face from executives.

Early Win & Proof Point Strategies

Designing for Initial Impact

Strategy 7

Selecting the Strategic Pilot

Imagine a team of incredibly talented architects. They've spent weeks evangelizing Event-Driven Architecture (EDA), successfully navigating the political landscape to get a green light for a pilot project. Excitement is high. They gather in a room to pick the first project. One engineer suggests rewriting the internal document management system's notification service—it's a technical mess, and they could build something beautiful and event-driven. Another suggests a brand-new, cutting-edge service for real-time analytics that would be technically fascinating. They pick the analytics project. They spend three months building an elegant, loosely-coupled, and technically impressive system. They demo it to leadership. The response? A polite nod, a quiet "that's neat," and then the inevitable question: "So, what's next on the product roadmap?" The project was a technical success but a strategic dead end. The momentum they fought so hard to build evaporates, and EDA is quietly filed away as a "distracting science project."

You are here if...

- You've finally secured approval to try EDA, and now you have to choose the one project to prove its worth. The pressure is immense.
- You know that the fate of your entire advocacy effort rests on this single choice. Pick a project that's too big, and you risk a spectacular public failure. Pick one that's too small or irrelevant, and you risk a success that nobody cares about, dooming the initiative to obscurity.

- You're staring at a list of potential candidates, feeling a mix of excitement and terror, knowing that your next move could either launch a revolution or kill it before it even begins.

The core principle of this strategy is this: Your first pilot is not a technical test; it's a political tool designed to build momentum. Its primary purpose is not to be the most elegant or complex implementation of EDA. Its purpose is to deliver a visible, undeniable business win that makes everyone—from the junior developer to the CTO—sit up and say, "Wow, we need more of this." You are not just building software; you are building evidence. You are building a story. Every choice you make, from the scope to the team, must be in service of creating the most compelling success story possible.

The Action Plan

To select a pilot that acts as a powerful catalyst for change, you need a methodical approach. It's not about gut feelings; it's about strategic calculation.

Tactic 1: Find the VISTA Sweet Spot

Your ideal pilot project lies at the intersection of five critical attributes. I call this the VISTA model: Visibility, Impact, Scope, Team, and Alignment.

- Visibility: The project's outcome must be seen and understood by people outside your immediate team, especially by management and stakeholders in other departments. A backend refactor that makes developers happy is great, but it's invisible. A project that visibly reduces customer support calls or speeds up a process another team relies on—that has visibility. But be careful. You want positive visibility, not mission-critical visibility. Don't pick the checkout service for your first pilot. Pick the order-dispatch notification service. If the checkout goes down, the company loses money in real-time. If the dispatch notification is delayed, it's a problem, but it's a recoverable one.

- Impact: The project must solve a real, painful business problem. Don't invent a problem for your solution. Find existing pain. Is the finance team manually reconciling data between two systems every month? Is the marketing team unable to get timely data to personalize campaigns? These are problems with measurable business impact. Solving one of them doesn't just prove EDA works; it makes you a hero to another department, and you gain a powerful ally.

- Scope: The project must be small enough to be completed in a reasonable timeframe, ideally within one quarter (3 months). This is non-negotiable. Long projects accumulate risk, lose stakeholder interest, and are more likely to get sidetracked by shifting priorities. You need a quick win. The goal is to deliver value, demo it, and start the next phase while the success is still fresh in everyone's minds. Your pilot should be a single, well-defined workflow, not a complete rewrite of a legacy monolith.
- Team: The project needs a team that is genuinely enthusiastic about trying this new approach. You cannot force this. An unwilling team, no matter how skilled, will see every challenge as proof that EDA is a bad idea. Find the volunteers. Find the team that is already fed up with the old way of doing things and is hungry for a better solution. Their energy and optimism will be your greatest asset when you hit the inevitable roadblocks.
- Alignment: The project must align technically. Technical alignment means the problem is a genuinely good fit for an event-driven solution. Problems involving real-time notifications, state changes, integrating disparate systems, or workflows that need to be resilient are perfect candidates. Don't try to force EDA onto a problem that is better solved with a simple CRUD API.

Tactic 2: Become a Strategy Detective

A project that doesn't connect to the company's goals is a hobby. To get continued investment, your pilot must be seen as an enabler of the company's strategy. This is how you score high on the "Alignment" part of VISTA, and it requires you to do some homework.

First, become a student of your company's strategy. Read the annual report. Listen to the recording of the last all-hands meeting. What are the C-suite executives talking about? Are they focused on international expansion, improving operational efficiency, reducing customer churn, or accelerating speed to market? Your pilot's value proposition must be framed in these terms.

- If the goal is operational efficiency, find a process bogged down by manual work or clunky batch integrations. Frame your pilot as a way to "fully automate the X-to-Y data reconciliation process, saving 40 person-hours per month."
- If the goal is speed to market, find a bottleneck where multiple teams are tightly coupled, and one team's release cycle blocks another. Frame your pilot as creating a "loosely-coupled service that allows the mobile team to innovate independently of the core backend team, cutting their feature release time by 50%."

- If the goal is reducing risk, find a system that is brittle and prone to cascading failures. Frame your pilot as "introducing an asynchronous process that isolates failures, ensuring that a problem in the reporting module can never take down customer order processing."

When you talk to leaders, you're not talking about events, brokers, or schemas. You're talking about their goals. EDA is just the how.

Tactic 3: Define Victory Before You Start

How will you know if your pilot was a success? "It works" is not an answer. You need to define clear, measurable success metrics before you write a single line of code. This does two things: it forces you to be honest about the expected value, and it gives you a concrete report card to show stakeholders at the end.

Your metrics should be a mix of technical and business outcomes.

- Business Metrics: These are the most important for your stakeholders. Examples:
- Reduce average order processing time from 5 minutes to 10 seconds.
- Decrease the number of customer support tickets related to "missing order information" by 25%.
- Achieve a 99.9% success rate for real-time inventory updates during flash sales.
- Technical Metrics: These are important for proving the architectural benefits to your peers and technical leadership. Examples:
- Reduce the deployment time for the participating service by 40%.
- Eliminate all synchronous dependencies between Service A and Service B.
- Demonstrate that the new service can handle a 5x increase in load with no performance degradation.
- Team Metrics (Qualitative): Don't underestimate the power of developer happiness.
- Survey the pilot team before and after. Ask them to rate their ability to work autonomously, the ease of testing, and their overall satisfaction with the development process. A glowing testimonial from a happy team can be incredibly persuasive.

Alongside metrics, you must also perform a pre-mortem and identify the risks. What could go wrong? What if the message broker performance isn't what you expected? What if the team struggles with the learning curve of a new paradigm? What if a key stakeholder leaves the company mid-project? Write these down and think through mitigation strategies for each. Acknowledging risks doesn't show weakness; it shows professionalism and foresight, which builds trust with leadership.

Common Pitfalls

- ✕ Avoid the "Big Bang" Pilot: Do not choose a project that requires you to rewrite a massive, critical part of your legacy system. The risk of failure is too high, the timeline will be too long, and you'll get bogged down in migration complexity. Your first pilot should be an addition or a small replacement, not a wholesale reconstruction.
- ✕ Avoid the "Invisible" Pilot: Do not choose a project whose success cannot be easily seen or measured by non-technical stakeholders. Refactoring a backend library or improving a CI/CD pipeline might be valuable, but it doesn't make a compelling story for a business leader. You need to connect your work to customers, revenue, or risk.
- ✕ Avoid "Undeclared War": Do not start a pilot with a team that is skeptical or resistant. You are introducing a new way of thinking, which is hard enough with an enthusiastic team. With an unwilling one, it's nearly impossible. Their resistance will become a self-fulfilling prophecy. Find the willing coalition first.

Key Takeaways

- ☞ Your Pilot is a Political Tool: Its primary job is to build momentum and prove business value. Every decision must serve this goal. Technical elegance is secondary to strategic impact.
- ☞ Use the VISTA Model: Your ideal pilot has high Visibility, clear business Impact, a manageable Scope, an enthusiastic Team, and strong Alignment with technical needs. If your candidate project is missing one of these, think twice.
- ☞ Speak the Language of the Business: Align your pilot with the company's strategic goals. Frame its success in terms of efficiency, speed, or risk reduction—not in terms of architectural purity.
- ☞ Define and Measure Success: Don't wait until the end to figure out if you've succeeded. Set clear, quantifiable business and technical metrics before you begin. This is your proof.

Further Reading

- Good Strategy/Bad Strategy: The Difference and Why It Matters by Richard P. Rumelt. This book is essential for learning how to think strategically and connect your technical initiatives to what truly matters for the business.
- Thinking in Bets: Making Smarter Decisions When You Don't Have All the Facts by Annie Duke. This book will change how you think about risk and decision-making. Selecting a pilot is a high-stakes bet, and this book gives you the mental models to place it wisely.
- Measure What Matters by John Doerr. A masterclass on using Objectives and Key Results (OKRs). The principles are directly applicable to defining and tracking the success metrics for your pilot project.

Strategy 8

Maximizing Pilot Project Impact

So you did it. You navigated the organizational maze, you made the business case, you used the VISTA framework, and you have the perfect pilot project lined up. It's a guaranteed winner. The team is fired up, and leadership has given you their blessing. The project kicks off. Two weeks in, a stakeholder sees a demo and says, "This is amazing! You know what would make it even better? If it could also generate a PDF report for my weekly meeting." It seems like a small ask, so the team agrees. A month later, another engineer realizes they could use a cutting-edge caching strategy that would make one part of the system incredibly fast. It's not strictly required, but it's a cool technical challenge. They add it to the backlog. The original three-month timeline comes and goes. The project is now in its fifth month, bogged down in report-generation bugs and the complexities of the new caching layer. The initial excitement has faded, replaced by a grim determination to just "get it done." When it finally launches, it's late, over-budget, and the initial, powerful success story is lost in a narrative of delays. The pilot worked, but the impact fizzled.

You are here if...

- You have the perfect pilot project selected and you're standing at the starting line, ready to go. The potential is enormous. But you know that the journey from a great idea to a celebrated success is filled with traps.
- You're worried about scope creep, technical rabbit holes, losing stakeholder interest, or simply failing to prove the value you promised.

- You know that choosing the right project was only half the battle. Now you have to run the race, and you can't afford to stumble.
- Your challenge isn't just to build the thing right; it's to execute in a way that creates an undeniable, magnetic success story that pulls the rest of the organization forward.

The core principle of this strategy is this: A perfectly chosen pilot can still fail; disciplined execution is what turns potential into proof. The strategic brilliance you showed in selecting the pilot gets you in the door. But it's the week-to-week discipline of focus, communication, and measurement that gets you the next round of funding. Your pilot project is a theatrical performance. You've already chosen a great script (the project) and cast the right actors (the team). Now, you have to direct the play, making sure every scene lands perfectly to deliver a standing ovation from your audience: the rest of the business.

The Action Plan

Disciplined execution isn't about rigid, bureaucratic processes. It's about having a simple, powerful playbook that keeps your team focused and your stakeholders engaged.

Tactic 1: Set Your GPS with OKRs

Before you write a line of code, you need to agree on your destination. The best way to do this is with Objectives and Key Results (OKRs). Don't get scared by the acronym; the concept is dead simple.

- An Objective is your destination. It's a memorable, qualitative statement of what you want to achieve. It should be inspiring.
- Key Results are the turn-by-turn directions. They are quantifiable metrics that tell you if you're actually getting closer to your Objective. There should be 2-4 Key Results for each Objective.

For your EDA pilot, you should have one, and only one, Objective. Remember, this is a focused effort. Here's what it looks like in practice:

Objective: Prove that our new event-driven approach can break apart our monolith to increase team autonomy and delivery speed.

- Key Result 1: Reduce the deployment time for the Inventory Service from 4 hours to under 20 minutes by the end of the quarter.

- Key Result 2: Eliminate 100% of synchronous API calls from the Orders Service to the Inventory Service.
- Key Result 3: Increase the pilot team's self-reported "ability to ship without dependencies" score from 2/10 to 8/10 in our end-of-project survey.

A quick but critical warning: Let's be crystal clear about one thing. OKRs are a tool for alignment, not for performance evaluation. The moment you tie an individual's bonus or performance review to hitting 100% of their Key Results, the system breaks. People will start setting safe, sandbagged goals they know they can hit, and all the ambition drains out of the process. OKRs are a compass to ensure everyone is pulling in the same direction. They should be ambitious, and it must be psychologically safe for a team to hit 70% of a really hard Key Result and call it a success.

Tactic 2: Ruthlessly Defend the Scope

Your pilot's greatest enemy is scope creep. It's a Hydra—a dozen "small," "easy" requests that will slowly strangle your timeline and dilute your impact. Your job as the advocate or team lead is to be the bouncer standing at the velvet rope of your project's scope.

The OKRs you defined in Tactic 1 are your guest list. If a proposed feature or change doesn't directly serve one of those Key Results, it doesn't get in. Learning to say "no" is a critical skill. But you can do it gracefully. Create a "Future Ideas" parking lot. When a stakeholder asks for that PDF report, you say: "That is a fantastic idea, and it shows how valuable this could be. For this initial pilot, we are laser-focused on proving we can get the real-time data flowing. I've logged your idea at the very top of our list for a future project, once this pilot is a success."

This response does three things:

- It validates the stakeholder's idea, making them feel heard.
- It politely but firmly rejects the scope creep.
- It reframes the rejection as a commitment to the pilot's success, which will unlock their desired feature later.

Protecting your timeline is everything. A win delivered in 3 months is infinitely more powerful than a "better" win delivered in 9.

Tactic 3: Run a Shape Up-Inspired Playbook

For a high-stakes, time-boxed pilot, you need a methodology that embraces constraints. The principles from Basecamp's Shape Up are a perfect fit. The core idea is simple but radical: fixed time, variable scope.

You work in fixed cycles, which are typically six weeks long. This six-week period is a non-negotiable container for the work. Before the cycle begins, you and the team decide on the appetite for a project—is this problem worth a small batch (1-2 weeks of the cycle) or a big batch (the full six weeks)? This decision sets the budget. The timeline is sacred. The scope is not. This completely changes how the team makes decisions.

Here's how to apply this mindset:

- Work in Cycles: A three-month pilot can be structured as two separate six-week cycles. This gives you a natural checkpoint halfway through.
- Empower the Team to Trade: The team is given the autonomy to make scope trade-offs to fit the work into the six-week box. Is the fancy caching strategy nice to have? Yes. Is it essential for hitting the Key Results within the cycle? No. So it gets cut. The team is constantly asking, "What is the simplest version of this that can ship on time and prove our point?"
- Use the Circuit Breaker: Shape Up has a powerful concept called a "circuit breaker." If it becomes clear that the project is not on track to finish within the cycle, you don't automatically extend the deadline. Extending time is the exception, not the rule. Instead, it triggers a hard conversation: what else can we cut to meet the deadline? This forces brutal honesty and prevents projects from becoming "zombies" that shamble on for months.
- Demo Progress Relentlessly: Even within a Shape Up cycle, the need for feedback is critical. You must still hold frequent demos for stakeholders. This ensures that the trade-offs the team is making are the right ones and that you're still building something the business actually values.

This approach turns the timeline into a feature, not a suggestion, and it's the ultimate defense against the gold-plating and scope creep that kill pilots.

Tactic 4: Build the "Success Story" as You Go

The most common mistake teams make is waiting until the project is over to think about how to present the results. By then, it's too late. The final report is a rushed afterthought.

Instead, create a living document from day one. It could be a simple wiki page or a shared document titled "EDA Pilot: Project 'Phoenix' Success Story." This document is your political ammo for securing the future of EDA at your company. It should be built out section by section as you progress:

- Week 1: The "Before" Picture. Paste your OKRs at the very top. Add the baseline metrics. What was the deployment time before you started? How many support tickets did the old system generate? Add a quote from a stakeholder about the pain they feel.
- During the Cycle: Add Evidence. Did a stakeholder say "Wow!" in a demo? Add the quote. Did the team have a breakthrough and solve a tricky problem? Write a short paragraph about it. Take screenshots of the new architecture diagrams.
- End of Project: The "After" Picture. This is the grand finale. Go back to your OKRs and put the final numbers next to the baseline. Add charts that show the "before" and "after" (e.g., a bar chart showing deployment time dropping from 4 hours to 20 minutes). Get a final, glowing testimonial from your key business stakeholder.
- The Lessons. Add a bulleted list of lessons learned. This shows honesty and helps the next team.

When the pilot is over, you don't have to scramble to create a presentation. You just have to clean up this document and share it. It tells a powerful, evidence-backed story of transformation that is almost impossible for leadership to ignore.

Common Pitfalls

× Working in a Black Box: This is the most common killer. If you don't show your work to business stakeholders frequently, you are almost guaranteed to build something that misses the mark. Constant, tangible feedback is your lifeblood, regardless of your methodology.

× Ignoring the Appetite: This is the Shape Up version of "gold-plating." The fixed-time budget is a feature, not a bug. If your team constantly argues for more time instead of cutting scope, they haven't embraced the mindset. The goal is to deliver value on time.

× Declaring Victory on "Code Complete": Your pilot is not a success when the code is pushed to production. It's a success when you have measured its impact against your OKRs and successfully communicated that story to the organization. The job isn't done until the "Success Story" document is in the hands of leadership.

Key Takeaways

- ☞ Execution Turns Potential into Proof: A great idea is just a starting point. The disciplined execution of your pilot is what creates the political capital you need to drive widespread change.
- ☞ OKRs are for Alignment, Not Judgment: Use OKRs to get everyone moving in the same direction. Keep them separate from performance reviews to encourage ambition and honesty.
- ☞ Fixed Time, Variable Scope: Embrace the constraints of a fixed timeline. It forces your team to make smart trade-offs, focus on what's essential, and build the momentum that comes from shipping on time.
- ☞ Build Your Victory Lap as You Run: Don't wait until the end to think about your success story. Document your progress, your wins, and your metrics from day one. A well-crafted narrative of success is the ultimate output of your pilot.

Further Reading

- 🕮 Measure What Matters by John Doerr. This is the definitive guide to OKRs. Read it to master the art of setting and achieving ambitious goals. It will fundamentally change how you approach any project.
- 🕮 Shape Up: Stop Running in Circles and Ship Work that Matters by Ryan Singer. This book provides the philosophy and techniques for shipping meaningful projects on time. Its fixed-time, variable-scope approach is a perfect methodology for executing high-stakes pilot projects.
- 🕮 Essentialism: The Disciplined Pursuit of Less by Greg McKeown. This book is a masterclass in the mindset required to defend your scope. It will give you the tools and conviction to say "no" to the good so you can focus on the great.

Strategy 9

Broadcasting Early Successes

You hit "send." The email, a carefully crafted summary of your team's successful pilot project, goes out to a list of stakeholders. It's all in there: the architecture diagrams, the performance metrics showing a 300ms reduction in processing time, the logs proving the new event stream works flawlessly. You and your team spent weeks, maybe months, getting this far. You solved complex technical problems, you navigated tricky integrations, and you proved that this new Event-Driven Architecture (EDA) approach actually works. You lean back, expecting the flood of congratulatory replies, the instant messages from curious colleagues, the meeting invite from your VP to discuss a wider rollout.

Instead, you get silence. A day goes by. Two days. Maybe you get a single, polite "Thanks for the update" from your direct manager. The momentum you worked so hard to build evaporates. Your pilot, a brilliant technical achievement, has landed with a thud, and you have no idea why. The organization just seems to shrug and move on.

You are here if...

- You've successfully completed a pilot project but are struggling to get anyone to notice or care.

- You're watching the window of opportunity close, and the enthusiasm your team had is starting to wane.

More specifically, you're here if...

- You know your pilot project delivered real value, but you don't know how to translate technical wins into a story that resonates with business leaders.
- You feel like you're shouting into the void, sending out updates that get lost in the noise of a thousand other corporate emails and notifications.
- You're not sure how to talk about your success with different groups. What excites an engineer is not what excites a product manager or a CFO.
- You see a risk that your successful pilot will become an isolated "science project" instead of the first step in a larger, strategic transformation.

The core principle of this strategy is this: A successful pilot that is poorly communicated is, for all practical purposes, a failure. The work isn't done when the code is deployed and the metrics look good. The work is done when the value of that success is understood by the people who can fund, approve, and champion the next step. Your pilot's results are just raw materials; your real job is to be the storyteller who shapes those results into a compelling narrative that builds unstoppable momentum.

The Action Plan

Broadcasting your success isn't about bragging; it's about strategic communication. It's an internal marketing campaign designed to turn a small victory into a catalyst for widespread change. You need to stop thinking like an engineer reporting data and start thinking like a campaigner building a movement.

Tactic 1: Don't Just Report, Launch a Campaign

A single email is not a communication plan. It's a single point of failure. You need a multi-channel, multi-format campaign to ensure your message breaks through the noise. This is your victory tour.

First, define your campaign goals. What do you want to happen next? Is it funding for phase two? Is it getting three other teams to adopt your new event-driven pattern? Be specific. Your goal dictates your entire strategy.

Next, map out your channels and cadence. Don't rely on email alone. A good campaign might look like this:

- Week 1 (The Teaser): A short, exciting Slack message in a company-wide engineering channel. "Big news from the Phoenix team next week about our work on the real-time inventory project. We've got some results we think you'll want to see."
- Week 2 (The Launch): This is your main event.
- The Email: Send a high-level summary email, but its main job is to direct traffic to more detailed artifacts.
- The Internal Blog Post/Wiki: This is the centerpiece. It should be visual, easy to scan, and link to everything else. Hint: Use the "Pilot Success Showcase" template (provided in the Resources section).
- The Demo: Schedule a 30-minute company-wide (or department-wide) demo. Record it. This is your single most powerful tool. Seeing is believing.
- Week 3 (The Roadshow): Take your message directly to key teams. Schedule 20-minute sessions with other engineering teams, product leadership, and any business units that were impacted. Tailor the presentation for each one (more on this in Tactic 3).
- Week 4 (The Follow-up): Share the recording of the demo. Post a link to the blog post again in relevant channels, perhaps highlighting a specific, interesting finding.

This approach respects people's time while creating multiple opportunities for them to engage with your success on their own terms.

Tactic 2: Translate Metrics into Money and Narrative

Nobody outside of your team cares that you reduced latency by 300ms. It's a meaningless number on its own. Your job is to translate that technical metric into a language the business understands: money, risk, speed, and customer experience. I call this translating for "money and narrative."

The "money" is the quantifiable business impact. You must connect your technical win to a business Key Performance Indicator (KPI).

- Instead of: "We reduced order processing latency by 300ms."
- Say: "We made the checkout process 300ms faster. Based on industry data, a 100ms improvement can increase conversion rates by 1%. This small change could translate to an estimated $X in additional revenue per year."

- Instead of: "We now publish an event every time inventory changes."
- Say: "By creating a real-time inventory stream, we eliminated the batch process that caused us to oversell products during flash sales. In the last sale, this cost us $Y in customer support calls and refunds. We have now eliminated that risk."

The "narrative" is the human story. Numbers are persuasive, but stories are memorable. Talk about the qualitative improvements.

- The Developer Story: "Before, the on-call engineer for the Orders team was paged an average of three times a week because of database deadlocks during peak load. Since the pilot went live four weeks ago, they have had zero pages related to this issue." This is a story about reduced stress and happier, more productive engineers.
- The Customer Story: "Remember when customers complained that they'd buy something, only to get an email an hour later saying it was out of stock? Our pilot fixed that. Now, the 'Add to Cart' button is grayed out the instant the last item is sold. The Customer Support team has already seen a 40% drop in 'out of stock' complaints."

Combine the money and the narrative. Lead with the story, and back it up with the numbers.

Tactic 3: Know Your Audience, Tailor Your Message

Sending the same message to your CFO and a junior engineer is a recipe for failure. Each audience has a different set of priorities, a different language, and a different "What's in it for me?" (WIIFM). You must tailor your communication for each one.

Here's a simple breakdown:

- For Executives (CEO, CFO, CTO):
    - **They care about:** Strategy, risk, cost, and revenue (the "money"). How does this project help the company win in the market? How does it reduce our biggest risks?
    - **Your message:** Keep it short, high-level, and focused on business outcomes. Use visuals like simple graphs showing a trend moving in the right direction (cost down, speed up). Explicitly connect your project to the company's stated strategic goals. If the company goal is "improve operational efficiency," frame your EDA pilot as a direct contributor to that goal. Avoid technical jargon completely.

- **Example hook:** "Our pilot for real-time inventory management directly addresses our strategic goal of improving customer satisfaction by eliminating the overselling problem that cost us over $200k last quarter."

- For Product Managers & Business Unit Leads:
    - **They care about:** Speed to market, customer experience, and new capabilities. How can this help me launch features faster? How does this make my product better for users?
    - **Your message:** Focus on agility and new possibilities. Show them how loosely-coupled systems allow their teams to build and deploy new features independently without waiting for other teams.
    - **Example hook:** "We've created a new OrderPlaced event. This means the Notifications team can now build a 'Track Your Order' feature without ever touching the core ordering service. They could ship that in two weeks instead of waiting two months for the next monolith release."
- For Other Engineering Teams (your peers):
    - **They care about:** Developer experience, reliability, reusable tools, and cool technology. How does this make my life easier? Is it stable? Can I use it?
    - **Your message:** This is where you can get more technical. Show them the code. Talk about the improved testability, the clear event schemas, and the better separation of concerns. Emphasize the "narrative." Talk about the reduction in on-call pain. Offer them reusable components, like a standardized library for publishing or consuming events.
    - **Example hook:** "Check out this new inventory-service. It's totally self-contained and communicates through events on our RabbitMQ cluster. We wrote a client library that handles all the boilerplate for you. No more direct database calls into our systems. Want to see the code?"
- For Operations, Security, and SREs:
    - **They care about:** Observability, reliability, security, and standardization. How do I monitor this? How do I secure it? Is it going to create a new kind of production headache?
    - **Your message:** Be proactive. Show them the new monitoring dashboards you built. Explain the security model for your event streams. Talk about how event schemas, defined with AsyncAPI, provide a clear contract that improves system predictability and reduces integration risks.

- **Example hook:** "We built a Grafana dashboard that tracks the latency and throughput of our new event stream. We also have alerts that fire if the consumer falls behind. All events conform to a schema in our central registry, so you always know exactly what data is flowing."

Tailoring your message isn't deceptive; it's just effective communication. You are highlighting the facets of your success that matter most to the person you're talking to.

Tactic 4: Create Lasting and Discoverable Artifacts

Your campaign will create a burst of energy, but you need that energy to have a long half-life. Slack messages disappear. Memories of a demo fade. You need to create permanent, easily discoverable assets that will continue to advocate for your project long after the launch week is over.

- The Central Hub: Your internal blog post or wiki page (the "Pilot Success Showcase") should be the canonical source of truth. It should be easy to find via your company's internal search. Don't bury it in a personal space; put it in a shared, official engineering or product space.
- The Recorded Demo: This is your most valuable artifact. Edit it slightly to remove any dead air at the beginning and end. Give it a clear, descriptive title. Post it to your company's video portal (if you have one) and link to it from the Central Hub. When new engineers join the company, you can point them to this recording as an example of modern engineering practices.
- The "Awesome List": If your pilot produced reusable code, patterns, or documentation, create a simple page on your wiki titled "Event-Driven Architecture Resources." Link to your AsyncAPI definitions, client libraries, best practice guides, and the Showcase document. This turns your project from a one-off into the foundation of a new standard.

These artifacts ensure that your success isn't just a story told once, but a reference point that guides and inspires future work.

Common Pitfalls

× Waiting for perfection. Don't wait until you have every single metric and a perfectly polished presentation. Communicate early and often. Share progress and early wins even before the pilot is "done." Momentum is a fickle thing; you have to build it continuously.

× Using a one-size-fits-all message. Blasting the same technical deep-dive email to everyone is the fastest way to get your message ignored by 90%

of the recipients. Take the extra hour to write three different versions of your announcement.

× Forgetting the "why." A list of metrics is not a story. Always anchor your results to the original business problem you set out to solve. "We did this to fix X, and here's the data that proves we fixed it."

× Claiming total victory too soon. Be confident, but also be humble. Acknowledge what you learned and what you'd do differently next time. This builds credibility and shows you're not just selling snake oil. Your pilot is one successful data point, not the end of the journey.

Key Takeaways

☞ Treat Communication as a Product. Your success story is a product you are delivering to the rest of the organization. It requires a launch plan, a marketing strategy, and different messaging for different user segments. Don't treat it as an afterthought.

☞ Translate Technical Wins into Business Impact. This is the most crucial skill for any advocate. Learn to speak the language of money, risk, and speed. Your job is to connect the dots so others don't have to.

☞ Stories Move People, Data Convinces Them. Lead with a relatable human story—the end of on-call pain, a better customer experience—to grab attention. Then, use your data and metrics to prove that the story is true and scalable.

☞ Make Your Success Discoverable. Your goal is to create a gravitational pull around your new approach. Lasting artifacts like recorded demos, showcase documents, and resource lists are the tools that create that gravity long after your launch campaign is over.

Further Reading

🕮 Made to Stick: Why Some Ideas Survive and Others Die by Chip Heath and Dan Heath. This is the bible for making your ideas understandable, memorable, and effective. A must-read for this strategy.

🕮 Storytelling with Data: A Data Visualization Guide for Business Professionals by Cole Nussbaumer Knaflic. This book provides a fantastic framework for turning dry charts and numbers into a compelling narrative.

🕮 Start with Why: How Great Leaders Inspire Everyone to Take Action by Simon Sinek. Essential for learning how to frame your project not around what you did, but why it matters for the organization.

Strategy 10

Communicating Early Failures

You know the feeling. It's a quiet dread that starts in your stomach and slowly climbs into your chest. You're looking at the pilot project's dashboard—the burndown chart is flat, the error logs are spitting out cryptic new failures, and the latest performance tests are, to put it mildly, a disaster. The deadline, once a comfortable point on the horizon, is now a speeding train, and you're tied to the tracks. The sinking realization hits you: We are not going to make it.

You are here if ...

- You're staring at a project timeline that has become a work of fiction.
- Your team is working frantically on a death march, fueled by the dwindling hope of a last-minute miracle that you know, deep down, isn't coming.
- You're caught in a terrible limbo, toggling between the professional duty to report the facts and the very human fear of admitting failure. Every conversation with a stakeholder feels like a lie of omission.
- Your one-on-ones with your team are a mix of forced optimism and shared anxiety. The pressure to just keep quiet for one more day, to hope something magical happens, is immense. But the fear of the inevitable, explosive discovery is even worse.

The core principle of this strategy that you must embrace is this: In a crisis, bad news does not get better with time. Hiding a problem transforms a technical issue into a crisis of credibility. Your single most important goal is no longer just fixing the bug or meeting the original date; it's preserving the trust of your team, your stakeholders, and your leadership. Proactive, painfully honest, and immediate communication is the only tool you have to protect that trust. Delaying the inevitable doesn't just make the problem worse; it makes you the problem.

The Action Plan

Navigating a project failure is one of the toughest leadership tests you will face. It's not about avoiding blame; it's about taking ownership of the situation and steering it toward a resolution. Getting this right can, counterintuitively, build more trust than if the project had gone perfectly. Here's how to do it.

Tactic 1: Call a Time-Out and Get the Facts

The moment you realize the project is off the rails, your first instinct might be to panic or to call an emergency meeting. Resist that urge. Your immediate emotional response is not a strategy. The first thing you must do is call a quiet, internal time-out. Your goal is to move from a state of "we have a problem" to "here are the specifics of our problem."

Your job is to become an investigator. Pull your core technical leads into a room and get brutally honest with yourselves. This is not a blame session. The only question that matters is, "What is the true, unbiased state of our project right now?" You need to gather concrete, undeniable data:

- What is the actual progress? Not what the project plan says, but what the code, the tests, and the working software show.
- What is the root cause of the delay? Was it an unforeseen technical complexity? An underestimation of a third-party integration? A critical flaw in the initial design? Dig past the symptoms. "The database is slow" is a symptom. "Our chosen NoSQL database struggles with the transactional query patterns required by the legacy billing service, a pattern we didn't discover in our initial proof-of-concept" is a root cause.
- What is the new, realistic forecast? Based on the data and the root cause, work with your team to build a new, defensible timeline. This can't be based on wishful thinking or a desire to soften the blow. It has to be a rock-solid estimate grounded in your current reality. Add a buffer for unknowns. If you blew your last estimate, your next one needs to be bulletproof.

Only when you have this data packet—the what, the why, and the when—are you ready to start communicating.

Tactic 2: Build Your Recovery Playbook

Walking into a stakeholder's office and saying, "The pilot is failing," is a career-limiting move. Walking in and saying, "We've hit a major, unexpected obstacle with the pilot. Here's exactly what it is, here's why it happened, and here is our three-point plan to fix it," is leadership.

Before you tell anyone outside your core team about the problem, you must have the solution formulated. Your recovery playbook doesn't need to be perfect, but it needs to be credible and show that you are in control of the chaos, not a victim of it. Your playbook should contain:

- A Clear Statement of the New Reality: "We will not meet the September 30th launch date for the inventory management pilot. Based on our current analysis, a realistic launch date is now November 15th." Be direct and unambiguous.
- A Blameless Explanation of the Root Cause: "We discovered that the latency in the event stream from the warehouse system is 10x higher than what was documented, which breaks the real-time guarantee of our service. Our initial tests didn't catch this because they used simulated data." This shows you've done your homework.
- A Confident, Actionable Recovery Plan: This is the most important part. Detail the concrete steps you are taking. "We have a three-part recovery plan: First, we are building a temporary caching layer to buffer the stream, which will take one week. Second, we are re-architecting the consumer to process events in batches, a two-week effort. Third, we are working with the warehouse team to find a long-term solution to the latency issue, but our plan removes them as a blocker for our launch."
- A Summary of Key Learnings: Briefly explain what you will do differently in the future to prevent this kind of issue. "Moving forward, all PoCs for projects involving external systems must include a mandatory stress test using a live data feed from the production environment." This shows maturity and a commitment to improvement.

Tactic 3: Communicate Up, Then Out

The cardinal rule of managing bad news is that your sponsor and key leadership should never, ever be surprised. They must hear it from you first, not through the grapevine or in a big meeting where they are put on the spot.

Your communication rollout should be deliberate and sequenced:

- Your Direct Manager/Sponsor: This is your first and most important conversation. Schedule a dedicated meeting. Walk them through your recovery playbook. This is a moment to show them that you are a reliable partner who can handle adversity. You want them to go into subsequent meetings as your ally, already understanding the situation and confident in your plan.
- Key Stakeholders and Dependent Teams: Next, meet with the leaders of any teams whose work depends on yours. These are the product managers waiting for your feature, the marketing team planning a launch, or the operations team preparing for support. Give them the same clear, confident message. The goal is to give them the information they need to adjust their plans.
- Your Own Team: Once leadership is informed, gather your entire team. They've been feeling the pressure, and they deserve the full picture. Be transparent about the new plan and the reasons for it. This is a critical moment for morale. If you handle it well—by taking ownership and presenting a clear path forward—you can actually boost their confidence and unify them around the new goal. They need to see that you have their backs and aren't going to throw them under the bus.
- The Wider Audience (If Necessary): Only after these key groups are informed should you update any broader status reports, wikis, or project dashboards.

Tactic 4: Master the Crisis Conversation

When you deliver the news, your tone and demeanor are just as important as the content. You need to project calm confidence, not defensive panic. Don't apologize profusely—that can undermine confidence. Instead, take ownership.

Use a simple framework for the conversation:

- The What (The New Reality): "I'm here to give you an update on the pilot. We've run into a significant issue and we need to revise our timeline. The new go-live date is November 15th."
- The Why (The Root Cause): "Let me walk you through exactly what we found and how we found it." (Explain the blameless root cause).

- The How (The Recovery Plan): "We have a clear plan to get this back on track. Here are the steps we're taking right now." (Present your recovery playbook).
- The Lessons (The Improvement): "We also learned something valuable here about how we validate dependencies, and we've already changed our process to prevent this from happening again."

End the conversation by opening the floor for questions. Answer them directly and honestly. If you don't know an answer, say so, and commit to finding out. Your goal is for people to leave the meeting feeling not happy about the delay, but confident that you have the situation under control.

Story Time

My first few months in Barcelona were a whirlwind. The city itself was intoxicating: the energy, the architecture, the late-night dinners. But the real thrill was the job. It was my first time on an international team, conducting every meeting, every code review, and every casual chat in English. The company was incredible, and I was determined to prove I belonged there. I felt a constant, low-humming pressure to be not just good, but exceptional.

I was assigned a key feature for an upcoming release. We worked in two-week sprints, and I confidently told my product manager, who was based in San Francisco, that I'd have it done by the end of the cycle. At first, everything went smoothly. But as I got deeper into the code, I started hitting unexpected walls. The complexity was far greater than I'd anticipated. What looked like a simple path was actually a tangled web of legacy dependencies.

The end of the first week came and went, and my progress bar was nowhere near 50%. Instead of raising a flag, I did what many ambitious but inexperienced engineers do: I decided to power through it myself. I started staying late. I took my laptop home, sacrificing evenings and weekends to wrestle with the code. In my mind, asking for help was a sign of weakness. Delivering the feature, no matter the personal cost, was a sign of strength.

But I wasn't making up ground. Every bug I squashed seemed to reveal two more. The sprint deadline, once a distant point on the calendar, was now looming.

As fate would have it, my product manager flew in from San Francisco for a week to meet with the team. He was sharp, friendly, and everyone respected him. His presence only amplified my anxiety. I kept my head down, typing furiously, hoping for a miracle. I avoided making eye contact during the daily stand-ups, giving vague, overly optimistic updates like, "Making good progress, should be wrapping it up soon."

The miracle never came.

On Thursday, the day before the sprint was set to end, I finally accepted defeat. My stomach was in knots as I walked over to the desk where he was sitting.

"Hey," I started, my voice barely a whisper. "Can I talk to you for a second?"

I explained that it wasn't ready. That I wouldn't be able to deliver it tomorrow. I braced myself for the worst.

I'll never forget the look on his face. It wasn't anger. It was a calm and profound disappointment that was somehow much worse. He was silent for a moment, and then he said, "Okay. Thank you for telling me. But please, don't ever do this again."

He didn't yell. He didn't lecture me about deadlines. Instead, he patiently started to explain the bigger picture. "Fran," he said, "when you finish coding a feature, you think your work is done. But from the company's perspective, that's when the work is just beginning."

He explained that for a major feature, the release is a starting gun for other teams. The marketing team schedules email campaigns and blog posts. The sales team is trained on the new functionality and might have already promised it to key customers with a specific delivery date. The support team needs to prepare documentation and get ready for a wave of new tickets.

"This time, we're lucky," he continued. "There wasn't a big marketing push planned around this. But if there had been? Your one-day notice would have been a disaster. We would have had to cancel campaigns and go back to customers with bad news, which damages our reputation."

He leaned in a little. "And the other thing is, we're a team. If you had told me last week, or even on Monday, that you were struggling, I could have managed expectations. We could have pulled another developer in to help you. We could have simplified the feature to ensure we delivered something of value. But by waiting until the last minute, you took all of those options off the table. There's nothing we can do with one day's notice."

It was a revelation. I had been so focused on my small piece of the puzzle (my code, my deadline) that I never saw the vast, interconnected machine I was a part of. My job wasn't to be a lone hero who silently carried the world on his shoulders. My job was to be a reliable cog in that machine, and reliability meant predictable, transparent communication.

That conversation was a turning point. I realized that in any team, everyone is trying to do their best work, and the biggest obstacle to that is a last-minute surprise. In a healthy organization, your colleagues are there to help you succeed, not to assign blame. My real failure wasn't being late with the code; it was being silent. I learned that asking for help when you're stuck is not a sign of weakness. It's a sign of professional maturity, proof that you see the bigger picture and trust your team to rally around a shared goal instead of an individual one.

Common Pitfalls

- × Avoid: The "Hope-as-a-Strategy" Trap. This is the most common and most dangerous pitfall. It's the voice in your head that says, "Let's just wait one more day, the team might find a miracle fix." Hope is not a plan. Every day you delay reporting a known, significant issue, you are actively eroding trust. The moment you know a timeline is compromised, the clock starts ticking on your credibility.

- × Avoid: The Blame Game. When the pressure is on, it's tempting to point fingers. "The DevOps team didn't provision the environment correctly!" or "The other team's API is junk!" This is a lose-lose scenario. It makes you look defensive and unprofessional, and it creates political battles that distract from solving the actual problem. Own the outcome, regardless of the cause. Frame it as "we" have a problem, not "they" caused a problem.

- × Avoid: Providing Vague, Non-Committal Updates. Giving updates like, "We've hit a few challenges, but we're working through them," is worse than saying nothing. It creates uncertainty and signals that you don't have a handle on the situation. Stakeholders will fill the information vacuum with their own worst-case scenarios. Be specific, even if the news is bad. "We are experiencing a 25% failure rate in our payment processing module" is a much better update than "We're having some issues with payments."

Key Takeaways

- ☞ Communicate Early, Communicate Always. Bad news ages like milk, not wine. Your primary job in a crisis is to be the source of truth. Delivering bad news early, with a clear plan, turns you from a source of problems into a trusted problem-solver. Surprises kill trust faster than anything else.

- ☞ Bring a Plan, Not Just a Problem. Never report a significant failure without also bringing a well-reasoned recovery plan. This demonstrates ownership, control, and foresight. Your stakeholders are less concerned with the problem itself than they are with your ability to manage it.

- ☞ Own the Narrative to Protect Your Team. When you take ownership of the failure at the leadership level, you create a protective shield for your team. It allows them to focus on the solution instead of worrying about who will be blamed. This builds immense loyalty and keeps morale from cratering. Handling failure well is a defining characteristic of a true leader.

Further Reading

- 🕮 Radical Candor: Be a Kick-Ass Boss Without Losing Your Humanity by Kim Scott. While the book is about management feedback, its principles of being "caringly direct" are essential for delivering hard news to stakeholders. It provides a framework for communicating difficult truths constructively.

- 🕮 The Phoenix Project: A Novel About IT, DevOps, and Helping Your Business Win by Gene Kim, Kevin Behr, and George Spafford. This book is a fictional but highly realistic look at an IT organization in perpetual crisis. It's a fantastic illustration of what happens when problems are hidden, blame is rampant, and no one understands the root cause of systemic issues. It will feel uncomfortably familiar and provides a great model for a better way of working.

Strategy 11

Building Trust with Clear Contracts & Documentation

Of all the promises of Event-Driven Architecture (EDA)—resilience, scalability, loose-coupling—the one that really matters day-to-day is the ability for teams to work in parallel without constantly stepping on each other's toes. This promise, however, lives or dies on one simple thing: trust. Trust that when you consume an event, it contains what you expect. Trust that the team publishing an event won't break your service with a silent, unannounced change. Without that trust, you don't have a loosely-coupled system; you have a distributed monolith held together with hope and late-night emergency calls. And that's a total nightmare.

You are here if...

- Your organization's approach to event documentation is "just go look at the producer's code."
- Your teams spend more time in meetings trying to figure out what data is in an event than they do actually building features.
- Every minor change to an event payload sends a shockwave of fear and uncertainty across multiple teams, leading to brittle, defensive coding and a complete paralysis of innovation.

You're here because you've seen firsthand that without clear agreements, your shiny, modern architecture feels just as messy and tangled as the monolith you were trying to escape.

The core principle of this strategy is this: An event is a public API, and it deserves a rock-solid contract. You would never let another team integrate with your REST API without providing clear, versioned, and reliable documentation through something like an OpenAPI specification. To do so would be considered wildly unprofessional. Yet, for some reason, when we switch to asynchronous communication, we often throw this discipline out the window. We treat events like casual, private messages instead of what they truly are: the formal, public interface of your service. Building trust in an EDA doesn't come from fancy brokers or complex frameworks; it comes from teams making clear, explicit promises to each other and then keeping them. These promises are your event contracts.

The Action Plan

Building a culture of trust through contracts isn't just about picking a tool; it's about adopting a new way of working. It requires a commitment to clarity, communication, and discipline. Here's how you can make it a reality.

Tactic 1: Make AsyncAPI Your Single Source of Truth

To build trust, you need a single source of truth that both humans and machines can rely on. For event-driven APIs, that source of truth should be an AsyncAPI file. The most important thing is that this contract exists, is accurate, and is an integrated part of your development workflow—not that you follow a rigid "contract-first" or "code-first" dogma.

AsyncAPI is the open-source specification for defining and documenting asynchronous, event-driven APIs. It's an idea I started many years ago to solve this exact problem, and it has since grown into a massive community-driven initiative.

An AsyncAPI file allows you to define, in a single, machine-readable YAML or JSON file:

- Servers: Information about the message brokers you connect to (e.g., the host, protocol, and security details).
- Channels: Where messages are sent and received (e.g., a Kafka topic, a RabbitMQ queue, an AWS EventBridge bus).

- Operations: What you can do on a channel, which is defined by an action like send or receive.
- Messages: The events themselves, defining their headers and the precise structure of their payload.
- Bindings: Protocol-specific information, like Kafka partition keys or RabbitMQ routing keys.

By making the AsyncAPI file the central artifact, you create the blueprint for development, code generation, testing, and documentation. Whether this file is written by hand before coding begins, or generated from code comments during the build process, it becomes the canonical description of your service's event-driven interface.

Tactic 2: Master Your Schema Design

Just using a contract format isn't enough; the contract itself has to be good. A poorly designed schema can be just as confusing as no schema at all. Your event payload is the heart of your contract, and designing it well is a skill. Here are the non-negotiables:

- Be Descriptive and Explicit: Field names should be self-explanatory. This is a perfect place to leverage the ubiquitous language from Domain-Driven Design (DDD). If your organization already has a well-defined ubiquitous language, you absolutely should use it. Naming your event fields (customerId, shippingAddress, paymentTerms) to match the established business terms is a huge win for clarity. If you don't have one, this is a great opportunity to start building one, even if it's just a simple company-wide glossary of terms. The goal is to avoid cryptic abbreviations (c_ts) or overly generic names. A field named customer_creation_timestamp_utc is clear because it's explicit. Don't use a generic data object that can hold anything; define the structure. A new developer should be able to understand the event's business purpose just by reading the schema, and using a shared language is the fastest way to get there.
- Think About Evolution: Your system will change—that's a guarantee. The most resilient way to handle this is to build Tolerant Readers. This is a pattern where consumers are designed to only process the data they explicitly care about and to safely ignore any fields they don't recognize. If a consumer only needs the orderId and totalAmount from an event, it shouldn't fail if the producer adds a new shippingMethod field. This approach makes your consumers incredibly robust and immune to additive changes. The producer's side of this bargain is to follow the golden rule: make changes backward-compatible whenever possible. This means only adding new, optional fields and never renaming or removing existing ones, as that would

be a breaking change. While the Tolerant Reader is the ideal, it has its own challenges. You may need to maintain a specific schema view for each consumer (what it needs) alongside the producer's complete schema (what it sends). This complexity can be managed, especially if you have automation that can map producers to consumers based on their contracts.

- Be Precise with Types and Constraints: A schema isn't just a list of field names; it's a promise about the data itself. Be ruthless with precision. Don't use a string for everything. If a value is a number, use an integer or number type. For dates and times, mandate a specific format like ISO 8601 (YYYY-MM-DDTHH:mm:ssZ) to eliminate ambiguity. Furthermore, explicitly define which fields are required and which are optional. If a consumer absolutely needs a customerId to function, the schema must enforce its presence. This level of precision prevents entire classes of runtime errors and saves every consumer from having to write defensive parsing and validation logic. It's a simple declaration that builds a huge amount of trust.
- Standardize Common Fields: Many events will share common concepts. Establish a standard for metadata that should appear in every event, such as a trace_id for observability, an event_id for idempotency, an event_timestamp, and the event_source service. This consistency makes the entire system easier to debug and understand.

Tactic 3: Implement a Clear Versioning Strategy

Sooner or later, you will need to make a breaking change. It's inevitable. Maybe a business requirement fundamentally changes, or you realize a major design flaw. How you handle this is what separates a mature, reliable system from a chaotic one. You need a clear and consistent versioning strategy.

There are two primary approaches, each with its own trade-offs:

- Version in the Payload/Header: Each event message contains a version identifier, like "event_version": "2.0.0". The producer starts publishing the v2 events to the same channel as the v1 events. Consumers can then inspect the version field and decide how to process the message.
- Pro: The channel name remains stable, which is simpler for infrastructure management. It allows for a gradual migration, as consumers can be updated one by one to handle the new version.
- Con: Consumers become more complex. They have to contain logic to handle multiple versions of the same event, which can lead to bloated code if not managed carefully. The broker can't help you—it will deliver all versions to all subscribers of that channel.

- Version in the Channel/Topic Name: When you introduce a breaking change, you create a brand new channel. For example, you move from publishing to order.created.v1 to publishing to order.created.v2.
- Pro: It's incredibly simple for consumers. A consumer subscribed to v1 will never see a v2 event. This completely isolates them from the breaking change. The routing logic is handled by the broker, not by the application code.
- Con: It can lead to a proliferation of channels or topics, which can be harder to manage and discover. You need a clear process for decommissioning old channels and ensuring all consumers have migrated before you can turn off the v1 publisher.

There isn't a single "best" answer; it depends on your context. The important thing is to pick one strategy, document it, and apply it consistently across your entire organization.

Tactic 4: Make Your Contracts Discoverable

A perfect event contract is useless if nobody can find it. You wouldn't hide your OpenAPI documentation on a developer's local machine; you'd publish it to a developer portal. The same applies to your event contracts.

Your collection of AsyncAPI files should not live in scattered, forgotten Git repositories. They need to be aggregated into a central, searchable Event Catalog or Schema Registry. This catalog becomes the go-to place for any developer in the company who wants to:

- Discover what events are available in the system.
- Understand what a specific event means and what data it contains.
- Find out who owns a particular event and who is consuming it.
- Get sample payloads and connection information.

The beauty of using a standard like AsyncAPI is that the ecosystem of tooling is already there. You can use open-source tools to automatically parse your AsyncAPI files from your Git repositories and generate a beautiful, human-friendly documentation portal. This portal isn't a nice-to-have; it's essential infrastructure for scaling EDA. It lowers the barrier to entry for new developers, accelerates integration work, and makes the entire system transparent and understandable.

Story Time

For a large European bank, moving to an event-driven architecture wasn't just a technical choice, it was a necessity. But it came with huge challenges. The complexity was immense, and meeting strict audit and regulatory requirements in a distributed system was a constant headache. Onboarding new developers was a slow, painful process filled with manual steps, and the lack of a clear, shared understanding of the system's event topology was crippling innovation.

They needed to move from a world of tribal knowledge and manual effort to one of automation, clarity, and trust. The solution was to build a complete, end-to-end workflow centered on a single source of truth: the AsyncAPI contract.

They adopted a GitOps approach, storing every AsyncAPI file in a central Git repository. This file became the "intent" for everything that followed. A change merged to the main branch would trigger a CI/CD pipeline that used the contract to orchestrate the entire system. The pipeline would automatically:

Generate broker topology: It read the AsyncAPI file and translated it into the declarative configuration for their message broker (Pulsar), creating all the necessary topics and permissions without any manual intervention.

Generate code and schemas: It produced server-side Java classes and JSON Schema definitions, ensuring the code was always in perfect sync with the contract.

Generate test fixtures: It pulled example payloads directly from the AsyncAPI file to create ready-to-use test fixtures, unifying testing across all teams.

Publish documentation: It rendered the contract into a clean, human-readable format and pushed it to an internal developer portal, making the system's APIs easily discoverable by everyone from DevOps engineers to business analysts.

By making the AsyncAPI contract the engine of their workflow, they transformed their architecture. What was once a complex, opaque system became transparent and auditable. Onboarding was radically simplified because the developer experience was now built around a discoverable, well-documented set of contracts. Most importantly, they built a system founded on trust, not just between services, but between the engineers who built them.

Common Pitfalls

Even with the best intentions, it's easy to stumble when implementing this strategy. Here are a few common traps to watch out for.

- × **Forgetting the Humans.** It's easy to get obsessed with making the AsyncAPI file perfectly valid for machine-readable code generation and forget its primary purpose: communication between people. A schema with perfectly typed fields but no description attributes is a failure. Encourage, and even enforce through linting, the use of human-readable descriptions for every channel, message, and field.
- × **Gold-Plating the Schema.** In an effort to get it "right" the first time, teams can fall into analysis paralysis, trying to design a schema that accounts for every possible future use case. This is a mistake. Start with the simplest schema that meets the immediate need. It's far easier to add new, optional fields later (a non-breaking change) than it is to build a complex, all-encompassing model that may never be fully used.
- × **Treating the Contract as a Manual Afterthought.** The most common failure mode is when a team builds their feature and then, just before release, manually creates an AsyncAPI file to "check the box." This completely defeats the purpose of the contract as a tool for alignment.

  Now, does this mean you must always be "contract-first"? Not necessarily. For teams with a lot of existing code, a "code-first" approach where you generate the AsyncAPI contract from your code can be a fantastic starting point. It gets you a contract quickly, makes your existing services discoverable, and lowers the barrier to adoption. It's a perfectly valid on-ramp.

  The real pitfall isn't the order (code-first vs. contract-first); it's whether the contract is an integrated part of your workflow or a one-off, manual chore. If you generate it from code, that generation should be an automated step in your CI/CD pipeline. The goal is to move away from a world where the contract is forgotten until the very end.

Key Takeaways

- ☞ Events Are Public APIs. Full Stop. This is the foundational mindset shift. Treat your asynchronous, event-based interfaces with the same discipline, rigor, and professionalism as your synchronous REST APIs. Trust begins here.

- ☞ Make the Contract an Integrated Part of Your Workflow. Whether you write the spec first, generate it from code, or do both, the contract must not be a manual chore done at the end. It should be an automated, repeatable part of your development and CI/CD process. This is the only way to ensure it remains the single source of truth.

- ☞ Good Contracts Are for Humans and Machines. A valid schema is necessary, but not sufficient. Use descriptive field names and fill out the description fields. Your primary audience is the developer on another team who needs to understand what you built.

- ☞ Discoverability Is Not a Feature; It's a Requirement. A world-class contract that no one can find is useless. Invest in building a central, automated, and easy-to-use Event Catalog or Schema Registry. This turns your collection of contracts into a living, searchable map of your entire system.

Further Reading

To go deeper on these topics, I highly recommend the following resources. They provide the foundational knowledge you'll need to master the art of building trust through clear contracts.

- 🕮 The AsyncAPI Initiative Website (asyncapi.com): This is the official home for the specification, tutorials, documentation, and a list of tools for code generation, validation, and documentation portals. It's the best place to start.

- 🕮 The Design of Web APIs by Arnaud Lauret: While focused on REST APIs, the principles of resource design, predictability, and focusing on the consumer's experience are universal. The mindset taught in this book is directly applicable to designing high-quality event schemas.

- 🕮 Building Event-Driven Microservices by Adam Bellemare: This book provides a practical overview of the patterns and principles for building event-driven systems, with a strong emphasis on the importance of schemas and contracts in managing a distributed architecture.

- 🕮 Martin Fowler's Articles (martinfowler.com): His blog is a treasure trove of wisdom on software architecture. Specifically, look for his writings on Event-Driven Architecture, Schema Registry, and the Tolerant Reader pattern, which is crucial for building resilient consumers.

Strategy 12

Implementing Incremental Schema Governance

The on-call alert screams at 2:17 AM. This story might be a fabrication, but I'm sure it sounds painfully familiar. A critical service in the billing department is failing, and it's taking the checkout process with it. Every minute of downtime costs thousands of dollars. After a frantic hour of debugging, the root cause is found. A completely unrelated team working on customer profiles decided to "improve" their UserUpdated event. They changed the userId field from a simple integer, like 12345, to a UUID string, like a1b2c3d4-e5f6-4a7b-8c9d-0e1f2a3b4c5d. They had no idea the billing service was listening, let alone that it expected an integer. The change, made with good intentions, brought a core business process to its knees. There was no contract, no warning, and no safety net. Just a silent failure waiting to happen.

You are here if...

- A small change in one corner of your organization has caused a major outage in another.

- Your teams live in fear of deploying changes because they don't know who might be consuming their data.
- The answer to the question, "What's the exact format of this event?" is a link to an outdated wiki page, a Slack conversation from six months ago, or worse, a shrug.

This is the messy, brittle reality of building distributed systems without a shared understanding of the data that flows between them. It turns the promise of loose-coupling into a nightmare of hidden, implicit dependencies.

The core principle of this strategy is this: Schema governance isn't about top-down control; it's about creating shared understanding and trust at scale. It's not a bureaucratic gate designed to slow people down. It's a foundational practice that enables teams to move faster and more safely. By establishing clear, explicit, and enforceable contracts for your events, you replace ambiguity and fear with clarity and confidence. The goal is to start with the absolute minimum process required to prevent chaos and then earn the right to add more sophistication over time. You don't need a perfect system on day one. You need a practical system by next week.

The Action Plan

Building effective schema governance is an incremental process. You start with a solid foundation and build upon it, always focusing on providing value and reducing friction for development teams. The objective is to make the right way the easy way.

Tactic 1: Establish Your Single Source of Truth

Before you can govern anything, you need a central place where your event contracts live. This is non-negotiable. An event contract, often defined in an AsyncAPI file, describes everything about an event: its payload schema, the channel it's sent on, and the servers it passes through.

Your single source of truth for these contracts should be a central Git repository. This isn't just a "good enough" start; it's a solid, powerful choice for several reasons:

- It holds the whole contract: Unlike many schema registries that only store payload schemas (like Avro or JSON Schema), a Git repo can host your complete AsyncAPI files, which include crucial context about servers and channels.

- Powerful automation: It allows you to leverage CI/CD pipelines (like GitHub Actions or GitLab CI) to run deep, custom validation checks on your contracts that go far beyond what a typical schema registry offers.
- Familiar workflow: Developers are already comfortable with the pull request workflow for code, making it a natural fit for collaborative contract reviews.

While a Git repository serves as your primary source of truth, you will likely use it in conjunction with a schema registry. Tools like Confluent Schema Registry, Amazon Glue Schema Registry, or Apicurio Registry are excellent for managing the lifecycle of the payload schemas themselves—handling versioning, compatibility checks, and providing efficient serialization for producers and consumers. The best approach is often to have your CI/CD pipeline automatically publish the payload schemas from your AsyncAPI files in Git to your schema registry.

Tactic 2: Define "Level 1" Governance: The Bare Essentials

Now that you have a home for your contracts, you need to define your initial, lightweight set of rules. The goal here is not to boil the ocean. It's to solve the most common and painful problems with the simplest possible rules. This is your "Level 1" governance framework.

Start with these three areas:

- Naming Conventions: Inconsistency is a breeding ground for confusion. Establish a simple, clear, and enforceable naming standard. For example:

  Event Types: UpperCamelCase (e.g., PolicyCreated, UserUpdated).
  Field Names: camelCase (e.g., policyId, firstName).

  This simple rule makes schemas predictable and easier to read for everyone.

- Standardized Common Types: Identify data types that appear in many events and standardize their format. This prevents endless debate and conversion errors. Good candidates include:
- Timestamps: All timestamps must be a string in ISO 8601 UTC format (e.g., 2025-08-05T19:54:00Z). No more Unix epochs vs. milliseconds vs. localized strings.
- Identifiers: All unique identifiers should be UUIDs.
- Country Codes: All country codes must be ISO 3166-1 alpha-2 strings (e.g., "US", "ES", "DE").

- Schema Structure with a Standard Envelope: Mandate a common envelope for all events. My strong recommendation is to adopt CloudEvents, a CNCF specification designed to describe event data in a common way. Using CloudEvents provides a consistent top-level structure with standard metadata attributes like id, source, specversion, type, and time. This is incredibly useful for routing, filtering, debugging, and general observability, as it gives you a consistent way to handle events regardless of their source or destination.

These "Level 1" rules provide a huge amount of value by eliminating the most common sources of ambiguity with very little overhead.

Tactic 3: Automate Enforcement in the CI/CD Pipeline

Governance without enforcement is just a suggestion. The most effective way to enforce your rules is to automate them. Your CI/CD pipeline is the perfect place to do this.

When a developer wants to create or update an event contract, they submit a pull request to your central Git repository. Your pipeline should automatically trigger a set of checks:

- Linting: Does the contract conform to your naming conventions and other style rules?
- Validation: Is it a valid AsyncAPI file? Is the payload schema valid in its chosen format (e.g., Avro, JSON Schema, Protobuf)?
- Compatibility Check: This is the most critical check. The pipeline can call out to your schema registry to determine if a proposed schema change is backward compatible. For example, adding a new optional field is fine. Deleting a required field is a breaking change that will cause downstream consumers to fail.

The pipeline should provide immediate feedback. If a change is safe, the build passes. If it's a breaking change, the build fails, preventing the change from ever being deployed. This moves the safety check from a post-deployment production outage to a pre-deployment automated step. It's a fundamental shift from reactive firefighting to proactive prevention.

Tactic 4: Make Discovery Easy with an Event Catalog

A schema registry is designed for machines. A Git repository is for version control. Neither is optimized for a developer who just wants to know, "What events are available and what do they mean?" For that, you need an Event Catalog.

An Event Catalog is a human-friendly portal for discovering and understanding your events. It should be the first place a developer goes to find out:

- What events exist in the organization?
- What business process does an event belong to?
- Who owns the event? (Which team is responsible?)
- What does the event's schema look like?
- Which services produce this event, and which services consume it?

A fantastic open-source tool for this is EventCatalog, created by David Boyne. The key is that the catalog should not be a separate, manually maintained source of truth. It should be configured to pull its information directly from your Git repository. When a new AsyncAPI file is approved and merged, it should automatically appear in the catalog, complete with documentation and visualizations.

By making events easy to discover and understand, you reduce duplicate work, accelerate onboarding, and foster a culture of reuse.

Tactic 5: Create a Lightweight, Federated Review Process

As your system grows, you'll need a process for reviewing and approving contract changes. The biggest risk here is creating a central "architecture review board" that becomes a bottleneck. Avoid this at all costs. Instead, implement a lightweight, federated review process built around your Git repository.

Here's how it works:

- Ownership: Every event contract has a clear owner, typically the team that produces the event.
- Review via Pull Request: All contract changes are proposed via a pull request (PR).
- Automated Checks First: The CI/CD pipeline runs all the automated checks first (linting, validation, compatibility). This gives the proposer instant feedback.
- Human Review: The PR is then reviewed by the designated owners of the event. For a new event, perhaps a representative from a central "platform guild" or a lead from a consuming team might also be invited to comment.

The goal of the human review isn't to check for syntax errors; the machines already did that. It's to ask bigger questions: "Does this event name clearly describe the business concept?" "Is this data really needed?" "Could this be combined with an existing event?"

This federated model keeps the people with the most context—the producing and consuming teams—in control, while the central platform team focuses on building the tools and standards that make everyone successful. It balances autonomy with alignment.

Story Time

During the writing of this book, I had a couple of chats with a domain architect in the API Competence Center of a large European bank, an organization with over 5,000 developers. For years, his team has successfully championed a mature, well-governed "API-first" culture. Any team wanting to build a new enterprise REST API goes through a well-defined process involving design reviews, automated linting with Spectral, and publication to a central catalog. This ensures their APIs are high-quality, discoverable, and reusable.

But a new challenge emerged, not from the top-down, but from the bottom-up. Feature teams, needing to build more responsive and loosely-coupled systems, started adopting Event-Driven Architecture on their own. The demand was real and growing. However, this adoption was happening in a vacuum. He described the situation as the "wild, wild world."

The process was simple and chaotic: a development team would go directly to the Kafka platform team, ask for a new topic, and get it. There were no standards. No naming conventions. No shared understanding of payload structures. No central catalog to see what events even existed. One team's customer_updated event looked completely different from another's, and nobody knew who was consuming what. This ad-hoc approach was creating a hidden web of brittle, undocumented dependencies, threatening the very stability and agility the teams were trying to achieve.

Recognizing they were already late, his team didn't try to boil the ocean with a massive, perfect governance framework. Instead, they took an incremental approach, aiming to bring the successful principles from their API governance into the event-driven world.

Their plan was a direct reflection of the tactics in this strategy:

- Establish a Source of Truth: They designated a central place where all event contracts, defined as AsyncAPI files, would live.

- Define Bare Essentials: They started drafting the "Level 1" guidelines: consistent naming conventions for topics and payload fields, standard formats for common types like timestamps, and a rule to use a standard event envelope.

- Automate and Federate: They began porting their existing API linting rules to validate the new AsyncAPI contracts in the CI/CD pipeline, providing instant feedback. The review process would be federated, managed through pull requests where the producing team and key consumers had a say, avoiding a central bottleneck.

- Enable Discovery: A key goal was to make these events discoverable in their existing developer portal, creating an event catalog so teams could stop reinventing the wheel.

Crucially, he noted they expected little resistance. This wasn't a case of architects forcing a new process on unwilling developers. The developers were already using events and feeling the pain of inconsistency. The demand for governance was coming from the feature teams themselves. They wanted the guardrails. His team was simply catching up to provide the structure needed to turn their chaotic "wild west" into a productive and reliable event-driven ecosystem.

Common Pitfalls

× Boiling the Ocean: Avoid the temptation to design the "perfect" governance model from day one. Don't start with a 50-page document of rules. Start with one page covering the absolute essentials. You can always add more rules later as new needs arise.

× Creating a Central Bottleneck: Do not create a single "governance committee" that must approve every schema change. This is the fastest way to make developers hate the process and find ways to work around it. Empower teams and federate responsibility.

× Forgetting the Humans: A schema registry is for machines. An EventCatalog is for humans. Focusing only on the registry or the Git repo is a common mistake. If developers can't easily discover and understand the events, your governance efforts will have a limited impact.

× Governance as a Punishment: If your process is seen as purely a gate that says "no," people will resent it. Frame governance as an enabler. It's a service the platform team provides to help product teams build more reliable systems faster.

Key Takeaways

☞ Govern for Trust, Not Control: The ultimate goal of schema governance is to build trust between teams. Explicit contracts, automated validation, and easy discovery are the tools you use to build that trust.

☞ Start Small and Automate: Don't try to solve every problem at once. Implement a few high-impact rules (naming, common types, standard envelopes) and automate their enforcement in your CI/CD pipeline. This provides immediate value and builds momentum.

☞ Separate Machine and Human Concerns: Use a Git repository as your source of truth and a schema registry for machine-to-machine interaction. Use an EventCatalog as the discovery portal for humans. All three are essential parts of a healthy ecosystem.

☞ Federate, Don't Centralize: Push ownership and review responsibilities out to the teams who have the context. The central platform's role is to provide the tools, standards, and guardrails that make this distributed ownership model work.

Further Reading

🕮 Designing Data-Intensive Applications by Martin Kleppmann: Chapter 4 provides an excellent, deep dive into schema evolution and forward/backward compatibility. It's essential reading for understanding the "why" behind compatibility checks.

🕮 CloudEvents Specification (cloudevents.io): Review the official spec to understand the standard attributes and benefits of adopting a common event envelope.

🕮 EventCatalog Documentation (eventcatalog.dev): Explore the website to understand what a modern, human-centric catalog can do. It will give you a clear vision of what to aim for.

Implementation & Scaling Strategies

Making EDA Stick & Grow

Strategy 13

Navigating Legacy Systems Integration

You've seen it. I've seen it. We've all seen it. It's the beast in the basement. The system that was built before many of the current engineers were even born. It might be a mainframe running COBOL, a giant monolithic application from the early 2000s, or a sprawling relational database that's become the company's defacto central nervous system. It has a name, often spoken in hushed, fearful tones: "Genesis," "The Core," or just "The Monolith." It's mission-critical, incredibly fragile, and nobody really knows how the whole thing works anymore. Yet, it holds the keys to the kingdom—the most important data and business logic in the entire organization.

You're here if...

- You've proposed a beautiful new event-driven service, only to be told, "That's great, but how does it get customer data from Genesis?"
- Your progress is constantly blocked by the legacy system's release schedule, which involves three weeks of manual testing and a weekend-long deployment window.
- Every new feature requires a risky, painful, and expensive change to this core system, and you know, deep down, that this is not sustainable.
- The business wants to move faster, but you're shackled to the past. The idea of replacing it is so massive, so terrifying, that nobody even dares to suggest it seriously.

The core principle of this strategy is: Don't fight the monolith; contain it. Your goal is not a risky "big bang" rewrite but a strategic coexistence where you gradually and safely transfer responsibility from the old system to the new. Think of it less like demolishing an old building and more like renovating it room by room while people are still living inside. You want to wrap the legacy system, listen to what it has to say, and slowly redirect the flow of traffic around it until it becomes a smaller and smaller part of your architecture. This approach minimizes risk, delivers value incrementally, and allows you to build your modern, event-driven future alongside the stable, functioning present.

The Action Plan

Integrating with legacy systems is a delicate dance. You need to respect the old system's role while preventing its old habits and technical debt from leaking into your new, clean architecture. The following tactics provide a proven, step-by-step approach to containing the beast and building your way out.

Tactic 1: Listen to the Source of Truth with Change Data Capture (CDC)

Before you can do anything else, you need data. The most valuable data is often locked inside the legacy system's database. The old way of getting it out—running batch jobs at night—is too slow for a real-time, event-driven world. The modern solution is Change Data Capture (CDC).

CDC is a technique that essentially lets you eavesdrop on a database. Instead of querying the database directly, a CDC tool taps into the database's transaction log—the internal journal it uses to record every single change. When a new order is inserted, a customer's address is updated, or inventory is changed in the legacy application, the CDC tool sees that change in the log and immediately publishes it as an event to a message broker.

This is incredibly powerful for a few reasons:

- It's non-invasive: You don't have to modify the legacy application's code at all. This is a huge win, especially if the original developers are long gone or the codebase is too fragile to touch. You're not adding any load or risk to the application itself.
- It's real-time: Events are published milliseconds after the change is committed to the database. This gives your new EDA services an up-to-the-minute view of the state of the business.

- It's the ultimate source of truth: You are capturing the data exactly as it was written, creating a reliable stream of facts about what happened in the business.

Your first step is to identify the critical data entities in your legacy system (e.g., Customers, Orders, Products) and set up a CDC connector, like Debezium, to stream changes from their database tables into your event bus. Suddenly, your legacy system isn't a black box anymore; it's a broadcaster of rich, real-time business events.

Tactic 2: Build a Protective Bubble with an Anti-Corruption Layer (ACL)

Now that you have a stream of events from the legacy system, it's tempting to have your new services consume them directly. Don't do it. Legacy systems have baggage. Their data models are often clunky, inconsistent, or contain fields that make no sense in a modern context (e.g., CUST_STATUS_FLAG_03). If you let this legacy dialect infect your new services, you're just building a new, distributed monolith with the same old problems.

This is where you need an Anti-Corruption Layer (ACL). An ACL is a dedicated service or component that acts as a translator or a bouncer between the old world and the new world. Its only job is to consume the raw, messy events from the legacy system and translate them into clean, clear, and well-defined events that reflect the language of your new domain.

For example, the CDC tool might publish a raw event that looks like this:

```
{
  "op": "u",
  "before": {...},
  "after": {
    "order_id": 123,
    "status_code": 4,
    "last_upd_tmstmp": "2025-08-05T20:52:20Z"
  }
}
```

The ACL would consume this event and, based on its internal logic, publish a brand new, clean event like this:

```
{
  "eventId": "abc-def",
  "eventType": "OrderShipped",
  "timestamp": "2025-08-05T20:52:20Z",
  "data": {
    "orderId": "123",
    "shippingDate": "2025-08-05"
  }
}
```

The ACL protects your new event-driven ecosystem. It ensures that all the services inside speak a consistent, modern language, promoting loose-coupling and making them easier to understand and maintain. It isolates the "mess" in one place, so if the legacy system changes, you only have to update the ACL, not every single one of your new services.

Tactic 3: Systematically Starve the Beast with the Strangler Fig Pattern

Listening to the monolith and protecting your new services is great for building new capabilities, but what about modernizing the old ones? The "big bang" rewrite is too risky. The answer is the Strangler Fig Pattern, named after a plant that grows around a host tree, eventually replacing it.

The strategy is simple in concept:

- Identify a seam: Find a single piece of functionality within the monolith that you want to carve out. A good candidate is something that is frequently changed, is a performance bottleneck, or is needed by many new services. Let's say it's inventory management.

- Intercept traffic: Put a proxy or an API gateway in front of the monolith. Initially, it just passes all traffic straight through to the legacy system. Nothing has changed for the users.

- Build the new service: Now, you build your new, shiny, event-driven inventory service. It manages its own data and communicates via events.

- Redirect: Once the new service is ready, you change the routing rule in the proxy. Any requests related to inventory (/api/inventory/*) are now sent to your new service. All other requests (for orders, customers, etc.) still pass through to the monolith.

- Repeat: Over time, you repeat this process. You carve out shipping logic. Then promotions. Then returns. With each new service you build and each new routing rule you add, you are "strangling" the monolith. More and more of its functionality is being handled by modern, loosely-coupled services. Eventually, the monolith might be handling so little traffic that you can finally switch it off for good.

This pattern turns a massive, scary migration into a series of small, manageable, and low-risk steps. Each step delivers value and can be tested independently.

Tactic 4: Guarantee Delivery with the Outbox Pattern

As you start building new services that need to both update their own database and publish an event, you'll run into a classic distributed systems problem: the dual-write. What happens if you save the data to your database, but then the application crashes before it can send the event to the message broker? You now have inconsistent state. The system thinks something happened, but the rest of the world never heard about it.

This is a trust-killer. To build a reliable event-driven system, you must guarantee that every change to your service's state will result in a corresponding event being published. The solution is the Transactional Outbox pattern.

Here's how it works:

- When your service needs to make a business change (e.g., update inventory), it doesn't try to write to its database and publish an event in two separate steps.
- Instead, within a single, atomic database transaction, it does two things: it updates the business table (e.g., the inventory table) AND it inserts a record representing the event into a special outbox table in the same database.
- Because this happens in one transaction, it's all-or-nothing. It's impossible for the inventory to be updated without the event record also being created.
- A separate, asynchronous process (which could be the same CDC tool you're using on the legacy system!) monitors the outbox table. When it sees a new event record, it reliably publishes it to the message broker and then marks the record as "sent."

This pattern moves the responsibility of publishing from your application logic to a reliable, separate process. It gives you an "at-least-once" delivery guarantee, which is the foundation for data consistency in a distributed, event-driven world.

Common Pitfalls

- × Forgetting the people. The biggest resistance to touching a legacy system is often cultural, not technical. There may be a team of "guardians" who have maintained it for years. Involve them early. Frame your project as something that makes their lives easier by reducing their on-call burden, not as something that makes them obsolete.
- × Boiling the ocean. Don't try to model the entire legacy system in your ACL from day one. Start with just the one or two events you need for your first new feature. An ACL that tries to be a perfect, complete translation of a complex monolith can become a monolith itself. Evolve it incrementally.
- × Gold-plating the data. Don't assume you need perfect, real-time, transactional consistency between the old and new systems for every use case. For a notification service, is it a disaster if the SMS arrives a few seconds late? Probably not. Accept eventual consistency where you can; it will make your life way simpler. Use the Outbox pattern where you truly need guarantees.
- × Underestimating the data migration. Moving the data from the legacy system to your new service (the first step in the Strangler pattern) is often the hardest part. It requires careful planning, scripting, and validation to ensure you don't lose or corrupt data in the process.

Key Takeaways

- ☞ Contain, Don't Fight: The goal is peaceful coexistence and gradual migration, not a risky, all-or-nothing rewrite. Your legacy system is not your enemy; it's a slow-moving partner you need to manage.
- ☞ Listen First: Use Change Data Capture (CDC) to non-invasively tap into the legacy database. This unlocks its data in real-time without forcing you to change fragile legacy code.
- ☞ Protect Your Future: Always place an Anti-Corruption Layer (ACL) between the legacy system and your new EDA services. This translator service keeps your new architecture clean, consistent, and loosely-coupled.
- ☞ Migrate Incrementally: Use the Strangler Fig Pattern to carve off pieces of functionality from the monolith one at a time. This reduces risk and allows you to deliver value continuously.
- ☞ Guarantee Your Promises: For new services, use the Outbox Pattern to ensure that every state change reliably generates an event. This is the foundation of data consistency and trust in your new ecosystem.

Further Reading

- "StranglerFigApplication" by Martin Fowler: The original, canonical article defining the pattern. It's a must-read for understanding the philosophy behind this gradual migration approach.
- "Anti-Corruption Layer" pattern description on Microsoft Docs: A clear and practical guide on the purpose and implementation of an ACL, often in the context of Domain-Driven Design (DDD).
- Debezium.io Documentation: The website for the leading open-source CDC platform. The tutorials are excellent for understanding how to put CDC into practice with different databases.
- "Building Microservices" by Sam Newman: This book provides excellent, in-depth strategies for decomposing monolithic applications, including detailed discussions of many of the patterns mentioned here.
- "Enterprise Integration Patterns" by Gregor Hohpe and Bobby Woolf: The definitive catalog of messaging patterns. While older, its patterns for transformation and routing are timeless and form the theoretical basis for what an ACL does.

Strategy 14

Managing EDA Complexity

You've done it. You sold the vision, you got the buy-in, and your teams are building services that communicate through events. The initial promise of loose-coupling and team autonomy feels real. The first few services are humming along, and developers are shipping features independently. It feels like magic. Then, one Tuesday afternoon, a customer support ticket lands on your desk: "A high-value order was placed two hours ago, but it's not showing up in the shipping system." The panic starts to set in. The order service says it sent the OrderPlaced event. The shipping service says it never received it. Or maybe it did, but the inventory service downstream failed to confirm stock, and the compensating event got lost. Where is the order? Which service dropped the ball? Suddenly, your beautiful, loosely-coupled architecture feels like a black box, a ghost in the machine. You're flying blind.

You are here if...

- The very autonomy you championed now feels like chaos.
- Debugging a simple business process requires a cross-team investigation that feels more like a crime scene analysis than an engineering task.
- Your developers are spending more time asking "did you get my event?" in Slack than writing code.
- You're worried that a single failed service could silently break a critical business workflow and you wouldn't know for hours or even days.
- The initial dream of EDA has met the harsh reality of distributed systems complexity, and it's a total nightmare.

The core principle of this strategy you need to internalize is this: In a distributed system, you cannot control everything, so you must observe everything. This is the fundamental mindset shift. In a monolith, you control the call stack. You can attach a debugger and step through the entire process from start to finish. In an Event-Driven Architecture, there is no single call stack. Control is an illusion. Your new foundation is observability. You must pivot from trying to prevent all failures—which is impossible—to building a system where you can instantly detect, understand, and recover from them. Your job is to make the invisible work of your system visible to everyone.

The Action Plan

Managing this complexity isn't about finding a single magic tool. It's about layering a set of intentional practices and patterns onto your architecture. It's about building the instrumentation for your system at the same time as you build the system itself.

Tactic 1: Build a Rock-Solid Observability Foundation

Before you do anything else, you must get the fundamentals of observability right. Without this, you are flying blind, and every other effort will be a hundred times harder. Observability in an event-driven world rests on three pillars, but with a unique, event-centric twist.

- Structured Logs with Correlation IDs: Plain text logs are useless in a distributed system. Mandate that all logs are written as structured data (like JSON). Every single log entry, for every service, must contain context. Most importantly, it needs a correlationId (or traceId). This ID is the golden thread that ties everything together. When a request first enters your system or a new process kicks off, you generate a unique ID. This ID must then be passed along in the header of every single event that is part of that workflow. When a service consumes an event, it pulls that ID from the header and includes it in all its own logs. Now, when you're hunting for that lost order, you can filter your centralized logging platform for that one correlationId and see the entire journey, step-by-step, across every service.
- Meaningful Metrics: You need two kinds of metrics. First, technical metrics for your messaging infrastructure: queue length, message throughput, consumer lag, and error rates. These are your system's vital signs. If the queue for the InventoryService is growing rapidly, you know you have a problem before it becomes a crisis. Second, and more importantly, you need business metrics. Don't just measure "messages per second"; measure "orders processed per minute" or "shipments confirmed per hour." Instrument your code to emit a metric every time a key business milestone is reached. This

connects your architecture directly to business value and helps you spot trouble in plain business talk.

- Distributed Traces: This is the absolute game-changer for EDA. While logs tell you what happened inside a service, and metrics give you an aggregated view, traces show you the entire end-to-end flow. A trace visualizes the journey of that correlationId as a timeline, showing which services received an event, how long they took to process it, and which events they published in response. It shows you the parent-child relationships between events, creating a map of the entire choreography. The industry standard for this is OpenTelemetry. By instrumenting your services with the OpenTelemetry SDKs, you can automatically propagate the trace context in your event headers and send this data to an observability platform. This turns your black box into a glass box.

Tactic 2: Tame Event Choreography with Sagas

Event choreography, where services react to each other's events without a central controller, is fantastic for loose-coupling. However, for any business process that involves more than two steps, it can quickly become chaotic and hard to reason about. How do you handle a transaction that needs to succeed or fail as a whole, when the steps are spread across multiple independent services?

The answer is the Saga pattern. A saga is a sequence of local transactions where each transaction updates the state in a single service and publishes an event to trigger the next step. The key to a saga is that it also defines a set of compensating actions for every step. If any step in the sequence fails, the saga executes the compensating actions in reverse order to undo the work that was already completed.

Let's take our e-commerce order example:

- Order Service: Creates an order in a pending state and publishes an OrderCreated event.
- Payment Service: Consumes OrderCreated, attempts to charge the customer.
- Success: Publishes a PaymentSucceeded event.
- Failure: Publishes a PaymentFailed event.
- Inventory Service: Consumes PaymentSucceeded, reserves the stock.
- Success: Publishes InventoryReserved.
- Failure: Publishes InventoryOutOfStock. This is a failure in the saga.
- Shipping Service: Consumes InventoryReserved and arranges for shipping.

Now, what happens if the inventory is out of stock? The InventoryOutOfStock event is published. The Payment Service needs to listen for this and trigger its compensating action: refunding the payment. The Order Service needs to listen for it and update the order state to cancelled.

Managing this requires discipline. You have to explicitly model and document these long-lived processes. You need to be sure that for every action that moves the process forward, there is a corresponding, well-tested compensating action that can move it backward. For extremely complex, multi-stage sagas (think 10+ steps), you might even consider a lightweight orchestrator—a dedicated service whose job is to track the state of the saga and issue commands—but for most cases, a well-designed choreography with clear compensating actions works beautifully.

Tactic 3: Design for Failure, Not Against It

In a distributed system, failure isn't an exception; it's a standard operating procedure. A service will go down. A network partition will occur. A message will be malformed. If you pretend this won't happen, your system will be incredibly brittle. If you embrace it, you can build a resilient, self-healing system.

- Idempotent Consumers: This is non-negotiable. Your message broker (be it RabbitMQ, Google Cloud Pub/Sub, or another) will, at some point, deliver the same message more than once. This is called "at-least-once" delivery, and it's a standard guarantee. If your consumer debits a customer's account every time it receives a ProcessPayment message, a duplicate delivery could be catastrophic. An idempotent consumer is one that can safely process the same message multiple times without causing a different outcome. You can achieve this by tracking the IDs of processed messages. For instance, before processing a payment, the consumer checks a database to see if that paymentId has been processed already. If yes, it acknowledges the message and does nothing. If no, it processes it and then records the paymentId.
- Dead-Letter Queues (DLQs): What happens when a consumer receives a message it simply cannot process? Maybe it's malformed (a "poison pill"), or it references data that doesn't exist. If the consumer keeps failing and requeueing the message, it can get stuck in an infinite loop, blocking all other messages behind it. A Dead-Letter Queue is your safety valve. After a configurable number of failed processing attempts, the message broker automatically moves the toxic message to a separate queue—the DLQ. This unblocks the main queue so that processing can continue. Your team can then inspect the messages in the DLQ to diagnose the problem without bringing the whole system to a halt.

- Retries with Exponential Backoff and Jitter: When a consumer fails to process a message because a downstream dependency (like a database) is temporarily unavailable, the right move is to retry. But retrying immediately in a tight loop is a terrible idea—you'll just hammer the service that's already struggling. The correct pattern is to retry with exponential backoff. Wait 1 second, then 2, then 4, then 8, and so on. This gives the downstream service time to recover. Add jitter (a small, random amount of time) to each delay to prevent a "thundering herd" of consumers all retrying at the exact same moment. Most modern message brokers and client libraries have built-in support for this. Use it.

Common Pitfalls

× Tooling Without Discipline: Buying an expensive observability platform but not doing the hard work of instrumenting your code properly. A fancy tool is useless if your services aren't propagating trace IDs or are still writing unstructured, context-free logs.

× Ignoring the Business Process: Focusing only on technical metrics like CPU usage or message throughput. If your dashboards are all green but customers aren't getting their orders, your observability is failing. Always tie your monitoring back to a business outcome.

× One-Size-Fits-All Failure Handling: Applying the same retry and DLQ strategy to every consumer. Processing a UserUpdatedProfilePicture event is not as critical as processing a ProcessPayment event. Tailor your resilience strategies to the business criticality of the workflow.

× Forgetting about Idempotency: This is a classic mistake that will absolutely bite you. Assuming "exactly-once" delivery is easy or guaranteed is a path to data corruption, duplicate charges, and angry customers. Build idempotency into your consumers from day one. It's not optional.

Key Takeaways

☞ Shift from Control to Observability: This is the biggest mental leap you have to make. Stop trying to build an unbreakable system and start building an understandable one. Your primary goal is to reduce the Mean Time To Detection (MTTD) and Mean Time To Recovery (MTTR).

☞ Make Invisible Work Visible: Use the "golden thread" of a correlation/trace ID to tie the journey of a single business process together across all your loosely-coupled services. Use logs, metrics, and especially distributed traces to turn your black box into a glass box.

- ☞ Embrace Failure by Designing for It: Failure is a given. Use patterns like idempotent consumers, Dead-Letter Queues, and intelligent retries to build a system that can gracefully handle the inevitable bumps in the road and, in many cases, heal itself.
- ☞ Model and Manage Your Sagas: For any multi-step business process, you must explicitly design how it handles failure. Use the Saga pattern with compensating actions to ensure that your processes either complete successfully or are cleanly rolled back, preventing inconsistent data states.

Further Reading

- 🕮 Designing Data-Intensive Applications by Martin Kleppmann: An essential, comprehensive guide to the fundamental principles behind distributed systems, including many of the reliability patterns discussed here.
- 🕮 Building Microservices, 2nd Edition by Sam Newman: Contains excellent, practical chapters on deployment, monitoring, and the Saga pattern in the context of distributed services.
- 🕮 OpenTelemetry Documentation (opentelemetry.io): The official source for the emerging industry standard in observability. Reading the specifications and instrumentation guides is time well spent.
- 🕮 "Saga Pattern" by Chris Richardson (microservices.io): A clear and concise explanation of the saga pattern, covering both choreography and orchestration-based approaches.

Strategy 15

Championing Internal Developer Platforms

You've done it. You've convinced a few teams to start building with events. The initial projects were a success, and now the idea of Event-Driven Architecture (EDA) is spreading. But instead of a beautiful, orderly garden of loosely-coupled services, you're starting to see something else grow: chaos. Team A is using RabbitMQ and hand-crafting their deployment scripts. Team B went with Google Cloud Pub/Sub but has a completely different way of handling schemas. Team C is spinning up their own message broker, and their monitoring setup is a total black box. Every new event-driven service is a brand new adventure in infrastructure, security reviews, and tooling. It's slow, it's inconsistent, and it's becoming a maintenance nightmare.

You are here if...

- You're seeing the promise of EDA get bogged down by implementation friction.
- Your developers spend more time wrestling with infrastructure YAML and security policies than they do writing business logic.
- Onboarding a new developer to an event-driven project takes weeks because they have to learn a unique, artisanal setup every single time.
- You're seeing the same mistakes being made over and over, and the operational overhead is starting to erase the very agility benefits you were promised.

- The "freedom" you gave teams has turned into the freedom to create a dozen different kinds of messes.

The core principle of this strategy is this: To scale event-driven development, you must make the right way the easy way. You need to stop thinking about infrastructure as a series of tickets and start thinking about it as a product for your internal developers. This product is often called an Internal Developer Platform (IDP), and its job is to provide a smooth, paved road for building, deploying, and operating event-driven services. When the official path is fast, safe, and well-lit, most teams will happily take it. You don't eliminate freedom; you offer a powerful, attractive default that accelerates 90% of the work, freeing up developers to focus on the unique business problems they were hired to solve.

The Action Plan

Building an IDP can feel like a huge project, but it doesn't have to be. You start small, treat it like any other software product, and focus on delivering real value to your first customers: your fellow developers by leveraging the amazing open-source ecosystem.

Tactic 1: Discover the Real Pains and Gains

Before you write a single line of code or a single proposal document, you must become an anthropologist. Your goal is to deeply understand the developer experience at your company as it exists right now. Don't assume you know the problems. Go find the evidence.

First, talk to people. Schedule 30-minute chats with developers and team leads from various projects, especially those building event-driven systems. Ask open-ended questions:

- "Walk me through the process of creating a new service that produces or consumes an event."
- "What was the most frustrating part of getting your last service into production?"
- "Where do you get stuck waiting for another team (like Ops, Security, or DBA)?"
- "If you had a magic wand, what's the one thing you'd change about how we build software here?"

Listen for patterns. Are they all struggling with boilerplate code for connecting to a message broker? Is everyone confused about how to register and validate event schemas? Are security reviews for new topics a known bottleneck?

Second, look at the data. Your ticketing systems, Slack channels, and support forums are gold mines. Look for recurring questions and support requests. Are there a ton of tickets for "Request a new queue" or "Help debugging a consumer group lag"? These are clear signals of common, repetitive tasks that can be automated. Analyze your CI/CD pipeline data. Where are builds failing? How long does it take for a code commit to reach production? Long lead times are often a symptom of infrastructural friction.

Finally, map the "developer journey" for a typical event-driven service. Whiteboard it out from "I have an idea" to "My service is running and monitored in production." Mark every step that requires a manual handoff, a ticket, a meeting, or a complex configuration file. Every single one of those friction points is a potential feature for your platform.

Tactic 2: Frame the Pitch Around Speed and Safety

Once you have your data, you can build the business case. A huge mistake is to pitch an IDP as a "cool engineering project." Nobody with budget authority cares about that. They care about business outcomes. You must translate developer pain into business pain.

Your pitch shouldn't be about "centralizing our broker tooling." It should be about:

- Accelerating Time to Market: "Right now, it takes a developer four weeks to get a new event-driven service to production because of manual provisioning and security checks. Our proposed platform will provide self-service tools to cut that down to a single day. This means we can deliver new features to customers, like real-time order tracking, months ahead of our current pace."
- Reducing Operational Risk: "We currently have five different ways of deploying and monitoring event consumers. This inconsistency makes it incredibly hard to diagnose production issues, leading to longer outages. A standardized platform provides built-in observability and alerting, reducing our Mean Time to Resolution (MTTR) and improving system stability."
- Improving Security and Compliance: "Each team is currently rolling their own security for connecting to our message brokers, which creates a high risk of misconfiguration. The platform will provide pre-approved, hardened components for authentication, authorization, and encryption, ensuring every service we deploy meets our compliance standards by default."

- Boosting Developer Productivity and Retention: "Our developers are spending an estimated 30% of their time on repetitive infrastructure tasks instead of creating business value. This is frustrating and a leading cause of burnout. The platform automates this toil, making our developers more effective and happier."

You're not asking for money to build a platform; you're asking for an investment to make the entire engineering organization faster, safer, and more efficient.

Tactic 3: Design the "Paved Road"

With your mandate secured, the focus shifts to execution. The goal of the platform isn't to be a gatekeeper; it's to be an accelerator. The concept of a "Paved Road" (or Golden Path) is your guiding star. It represents the well-supported, streamlined path for completing a specific technical task, like deploying a new event consumer.

The most powerful "paved roads" are those that automate infrastructure directly from the source of truth—the design contract. For EDA, this means driving your automation from the AsyncAPI file. Instead of building a separate UI or CLI just to request a new topic, you integrate this process into the developer's natural workflow: Git.

Here's how this advanced, contract-driven provisioning works:

- A developer needs a new topic. They don't fill out a ticket or go to a portal. They open their service's asyncapi.yaml file.
- They define the change in the contract. They add a new channel to their AsyncAPI definition, detailing its name, the messages it will carry, its bindings, and, potentially, its custom extensions. These bindings and extensions are key, as they can carry the protocol-specific details (like Kafka partition settings) or platform-specific metadata (like an owner's team name) that your automation scripts will need.
- They open a Pull Request (PR). This is the crucial control gate. The change is now visible and version-controlled.
- CI/CD automation kicks in. The platform's CI/CD pipeline detects the change to the AsyncAPI file in the PR. It automatically validates the file and, critically, provisions the corresponding topic in your development and testing environments. The developer can immediately start testing their code against a real, working topic.

- The right people are notified. The same CI/CD job automatically tags the platform or Ops team as a mandatory reviewer on the PR. They don't review a ticket; they review the contract change directly in the Git platform they already use.
- Approval and merge trigger production. Once the PR is reviewed, approved, and merged into the main branch, the CI/CD pipeline runs again. This time, it provisions the topic in the production broker.

This GitOps approach is incredibly powerful. The AsyncAPI file becomes the executable source of truth for both humans and machines. It drives documentation, code generation, and now, the infrastructure itself.

Your paved road for EDA should be a collection of these kinds of integrated experiences:

- Contract-Driven Provisioning: The GitOps workflow described above for managing broker resources. This is the cornerstone of your platform.
- Service Scaffolding: Instead of building a whole new CLI from scratch, leverage the fantastic open-source tools that already exist. You can use the official AsyncAPI CLI and focus your efforts on creating a custom generator template for your company. With a single command like asyncapi generate fromTemplate asyncapi.yaml ./my-company-template -o ./new-service, a developer can get a complete, production-ready service skeleton with your company's best practices already built-in: the right libraries, connection logic, observability hooks, and even the CI/CD pipeline file ready to go.
- A Discoverability Portal: To untangle the messy web of services, you need a dedicated catalog. EventCatalog ****is designed for this exact purpose. You can set up a pipeline to automatically feed it all the asyncapi.yaml files from your repositories. It then gives you a powerful UI to visualize your architecture, see how events flow between services, and allow developers to easily discover and understand the events available to them.
- An Observability Portal: While discoverability is about understanding the architecture, observability is about understanding its real-time health. This is where a tool like Backstage shines. You can build a portal that pulls together all the operational views for a given service—metrics dashboards from Prometheus, logs from Splunk, traces from Jaeger—into a single, unified "pane of glass." A developer can go from the EventCatalog to see what a service should do, then click straight through to a Backstage portal to see what it is doing in production.

Tactic 4: Standardize the Core, Empower the Edge

A common fear with platforms is that they will stifle innovation and force a one-size-fits-all solution on everyone. This is a legitimate concern. The key is to find the right balance between standardization and flexibility.

The rule is simple: standardize the things that provide leverage, and allow flexibility on things that don't.

- Standardize the Core: These are the non-negotiables that ensure safety, security, and interoperability. Things like:
    - How services authenticate to the message broker.
    - The format for structured logs.
    - The location of the central schema registry.
    - The mechanism for exporting metrics and traces.
    - These things should be baked into the platform's templates and automated workflows.
- Empower the Edge: This is about choice. If you go off-road from the paved path, you are responsible for your own support. For instance, your custom AsyncAPI generator template might be for Go services. If a team wants to use Rust, they are free to do so, but they will have to create their own service from scratch and ensure it meets the core standards (like structured logging) on their own. This approach makes the platform an attractive choice rather than a mandate.

Common Pitfalls

× Building the platform in an ivory tower. If you don't solve your developers' most pressing, tangible problems first, you'll build a beautiful, expensive platform that nobody wants to use. Start with their pain.

× Making adoption mandatory from day one. Your platform must earn its users by being demonstrably better. Start with pilot teams and let word-of-mouth be your marketing. Forcing it creates resentment.

× Building what you can adopt. Don't fall into the "Not Invented Here" syndrome. The open-source ecosystem for developer platforms is incredible. Use tools like the AsyncAPI CLI, EventCatalog, and Backstage instead of building everything from scratch. Focus your unique effort on the templates and glue code that capture your company's best practices.

× Forgetting the "product" mindset. A platform is not a one-and-done project. It's a living product that needs a roadmap, user feedback channels, and ongoing maintenance. Treat it like one.

Key Takeaways

☞ Treat your platform as a product, not a project. Your customers are your internal developers. Your goal is to make their lives easier by solving their biggest points of friction.

☞ Automate from the contract. Use the AsyncAPI file as the single source of truth to drive everything: service scaffolding, infrastructure provisioning, and documentation. This creates a powerful, consistent GitOps workflow.

☞ Leverage the open-source ecosystem. Don't reinvent the wheel. Use tools like the AsyncAPI CLI, EventCatalog, and Backstage as the foundation of your platform and focus your energy on configuring them for your specific needs.

☞ Start small and iterate. Find the biggest pain point, deliver a small solution that provides immediate value (like a service template or an automated CI job), and then build momentum from there.

Further Reading

🕮 Team Topologies: Organizing Business and Technology Teams for Fast Flow by Matthew Skelton and Manuel Pais. The foundational text for understanding platform teams as a way to reduce cognitive load and enable fast flow.

🕮 The AsyncAPI Website (asyncapi.com): Specifically, dive into the documentation for the CLI and the Generator tool. Understanding how to build a custom template is the key to the service scaffolding strategy.

🕮 EventCatalog (eventcatalog.dev): The official site for David Boyne's excellent tool. The documentation and examples are the best way to understand how to set up a discoverability portal.

🕮 Backstage (backstage.io): The CNCF project for building developer portals. Explore their documentation to see how you can unify tooling and create a "single pane of glass" for your developers.

Strategy 16

Establishing Practical EDA Governance

You've done it. You championed the move to an Event-Driven Architecture (EDA), you won the arguments, and you even got a few pilot projects off the ground. Teams are excited. They're building new, loosely-coupled services, publishing events, and consuming them. For a moment, everything feels like it's working. The initial velocity is intoxicating. But then, a few months later, the cracks start to show. The on-call engineer for the Shipping team gets paged at 2 AM because their service is throwing errors. After a frantic hour of debugging, they discover the cause: the Payments team, without any announcement, added a new required field to the OrderProcessed event. The Shipping service, not knowing how to handle it, crashed. The next day, you discover two new teams are both working on a CustomerUpdated event, but with completely different schemas and for different purposes. One team calls it CustomerModified, the other calls it CustomerProfileUpdated. It's chaos.

You are here if...

- The initial excitement of EDA has given way to a growing sense of disorder.
- You're seeing services break because of unexpected event changes.
- You find duplicate or near-duplicate events popping up across the organization, creating confusion and wasted effort.

- Nobody is quite sure who owns a particular event stream or who to talk to before making a change.
- Security reviews for new event-driven services are becoming a bottleneck because there are no clear standards to check against.
- Your promising, loosely-coupled paradise is starting to look a lot like the tightly-coupled mess you were trying to escape, just with a message broker in the middle.
- You've traded a visible, monolithic dependency graph for an invisible, chaotic web of events.
- You've entered the "Wild West" of EDA, and you realize that without some rules, you're on a fast track to building a distributed monolith.

The core principle of this strategy is this: Practical governance enables speed and autonomy by making the right way the easy way. Forget the image of governance as a slow, bureaucratic committee that exists only to say "no." That's old-world thinking. In the context of modern, distributed systems, governance isn't about control; it's about enablement. It's not about building gates that stop developers in their tracks; it's about paving a superhighway with clear lanes, signposts, and guardrails. When the path to building a compliant, secure, and discoverable event-driven service is easier than going off-road, teams will naturally follow it. Good governance removes ambiguity and cognitive load, freeing up teams to focus on delivering business value instead of reinventing the wheel or cleaning up messes.

The Action Plan

To move from chaos to clarity, you need a deliberate, practical approach to governance. This isn't about writing a 100-page document that nobody will read. It's about establishing a lightweight framework and automating as much of it as possible.

Tactic 1: Define Your Core Governance Domains

Before you can create rules, you have to know what you're governing. Don't try to boil the ocean. Focus on the four areas that cause the most pain when left unmanaged.

- Event Design: This is about the structure and semantics of your events. It's the shared language of your entire architecture. If you don't get this right, nothing else matters. You need to establish clear, simple conventions for:
- Naming: How will you name your events and channels (or topics)? A common and effective pattern is Noun-VerbInPastTense, like OrderShipped

or CustomerRegistered. For channels, you might use a dot-notation that includes the domain, like shipping.orders.v1. Whatever you choose, be consistent.

- Payload Structure: What does the data inside the event look like? Will you have a common envelope with metadata like a traceId, source, and timestamp? What about the actual business data? Standardizing this prevents every consumer from having to parse a completely different structure.

- Granularity: Should you have one big CustomerUpdated event with 50 fields, or smaller, more specific events like CustomerAddressChanged and CustomerPaymentMethodAdded? The answer is usually the latter (smaller, more focused events), but you need to provide guidance.

- Schema Management: Schemas are the contracts of your EDA. They define the precise structure and data types for an event. Managing them is non-negotiable.

- Schema Format: Will you use JSON Schema, Avro, or Protobuf? Pick one standard format to avoid chaos. I'm partial to JSON Schema because of its widespread use and readability, and it's the default for AsyncAPI.

- Versioning: This is critical. How will you handle changes to an event schema? You absolutely must use a clear versioning strategy, like Semantic Versioning (SemVer), and enforce rules for backward and forward compatibility. A breaking change (e.g., removing a field or changing a data type) must result in a major version bump (e.g., from v1 to v2).

- Schema Registry: Where will schemas live? A central schema registry is essential. It acts as the single source of truth for all event contracts in your organization. This is where developers go to find out what an event looks like and where your automation tools go to validate schemas.

- Ownership: An event without a clear owner is an orphan. When something goes wrong or a change is needed, nobody knows who to call. Every single event and service must have a designated owning team. This owner is responsible for the event's entire lifecycle: defining its schema, ensuring its quality, managing its evolution, and eventually, retiring it. This isn't about blame; it's about accountability and creating clear communication paths.

- Security: In a request-response world, you secure endpoints. In an event-driven world, you secure channels and events. You need to define your security policies upfront.

- Authentication & Authorization: Which services are allowed to publish to a specific channel? Which are allowed to subscribe? This needs to be defined and enforced at the broker level (e.g., using policies in AWS EventBridge or user permissions in RabbitMQ).

- Data Classification: Not all data is equal. An OrderShipped event might contain Personally Identifiable Information (PII) and needs to be handled differently than a generic InventoryScanned event. Create a simple classification system (e.g., Public, Internal, Confidential) and define handling rules for each.
- Encryption: Is data encrypted in transit? At rest? Your security policy should state the requirements clearly.

Tactic 2: Choose Your Governance Model

Once you know what you need to govern, you need to decide how you'll make decisions and enforce the rules. There are three common models, and the right one for you depends on your organization's size, culture, and maturity.

- Centralized Model: A single, central team (often called a "Platform Team" or "Center of Excellence") defines all the standards, provides the core tooling, and reviews all new events and services for compliance.
- Pros: High consistency and control. Easiest to implement in smaller organizations or highly regulated industries where standardization is paramount.
- Cons: Can quickly become a bottleneck as the organization grows. The central team can become an "ivory tower," detached from the daily realities of development teams. This model scales poorly.
- Federated Model: A central body establishes a lightweight, "constitutional" framework (the core principles and tools), but delegates the responsibility for creating and enforcing domain-specific standards to the domains themselves. Each business domain (e.g., "Shipping," "Payments," "Marketing") has the autonomy to manage its own events, as long as they operate within the shared guardrails.
- Pros: Highly scalable and promotes autonomy and ownership. Empowers teams and avoids bottlenecks.
- Cons: Can lead to inconsistencies if the central framework isn't strong enough. Requires a higher level of maturity in the domain teams.
- Hybrid Model: This is often the sweet spot and the most common successful pattern. A central platform team owns the "what" and the "how"—the core infrastructure (brokers, registries), the universal standards (naming conventions, security baselines), and the automated tooling (CI checks,

linters). The domain teams own the "content"—the business logic, the specific event schemas, and the service implementation. They operate with high autonomy within the paved road provided by the central team. This model balances consistency with speed.

Tactic 3: Establish Clear Roles and Decision Flows

Whatever model you choose, people need to know who is responsible for what. Ambiguity here leads to inaction or chaos. Define a few key roles.

- Event Owner: The team responsible for the business capability that produces the event. They own the schema, the data quality, and the lifecycle of that event.

- Platform Team: The team that owns the EDA infrastructure (the message brokers, schema registry, developer portal). They provide the "paved road" for other teams to use.

- Governance Guild (or Council): This is a virtual team, not a formal organizational unit. It's composed of representatives from the platform team and the various development teams across different domains. This group is responsible for evolving the governance standards over time. They meet regularly to discuss challenges, propose changes to the conventions, and ensure the governance framework is actually helping, not hindering, developers. This is the beating heart of a federated or hybrid model.

Your decision-making flow should be clear. For example: A developer wants to create a new event.

- They use a standardized AsyncAPI template provided by the Platform Team.

- They define their schema, following the documented naming and design conventions.

- They submit their AsyncAPI file in a pull request.

- An automated CI pipeline job runs, linting the file against the governance rules.

- If the checks pass, the schema is automatically registered, and the required channel and permissions on the broker (like Google Cloud Pub/Sub or ActiveMQ) are provisioned.

- Human review is only required for exceptional cases, like a major version change that could break consumers.

Tactic 4: Automate Governance to Make It Invisible

This is the most important tactic for making governance practical. Manual reviews don't scale and are prone to error. The goal is to embed your governance rules directly into the developer workflow.

- Lint Your Definitions: Use a tool like Spectral to create a ruleset that automatically checks your AsyncAPI or OpenAPI files. You can enforce naming conventions, require certain metadata fields (like an owner field), and check for versioning best practices. Run this linter as a pre-commit hook and in your CI pipeline. If a definition doesn't comply, the build fails. This provides immediate feedback to the developer.
- Automate Schema Compatibility Checks: When a team proposes a change to an existing event schema, your CI pipeline should automatically pull the previous version from the schema registry and run a compatibility check. If a change is backward-incompatible but isn't marked as a new major version, the build should fail. This prevents the 2 AM "the event broke my service" scenario.
- Codify Your Infrastructure: Use Infrastructure as Code (IaC) tools like Terraform or CloudFormation to manage your broker configuration. The creation of topics, queues, and permissions shouldn't be a manual process done through a UI. It should be defined in code, reviewed, and deployed through a pipeline, ensuring consistency and auditability.
- Generate Everything: The AsyncAPI file should be your single source of truth. From it, you can automatically generate documentation for your developer portal, client and server code in various languages, and even the Terraform configuration for the broker. When you automate generation, you ensure that your code, documentation, and infrastructure are always in sync with your contract.

Common Pitfalls

× Avoid: Creating an Ivory Tower. Don't let a central team or architectural committee define standards in a vacuum. The rules you create must be grounded in the reality of the developers who will use them. The Governance Guild model is a great way to prevent this, as the people defining the standards are also the ones who have to live with them.

× Avoid: Manual Enforcement. If your governance strategy relies on people remembering to follow rules written in a Confluence page, it will fail. Humans forget, take shortcuts, and make mistakes. Automate every check you possibly can. Governance should be a seatbelt that's always on, not a checklist you fill out once in a while.

- × Avoid: Aiming for Perfection from Day One. Don't try to define every possible rule for every possible scenario before you start. Begin with the basics: a consistent naming convention, a schema registry, and ownership. Start there, automate it, and let your Governance Guild evolve the standards over time based on real-world challenges.

- × Avoid: Governance as a Weapon. The goal of governance is to enable, not to punish. The language you use matters. It's not about "passing an audit"; it's about "making our systems more resilient." The tools should provide helpful, immediate feedback, not shaming developers for making a mistake.

Key Takeaways

- ☞ Governance is an Enabler, Not a Blocker: Shift your mindset. The purpose of EDA governance is to increase developer autonomy and velocity by providing a safe, clear, and efficient path for building event-driven systems.

- ☞ Start with the Core Four: Don't get overwhelmed. Focus your initial efforts on the four areas that deliver the most value: Event Design, Schema Management, Ownership, and Security. Get these right, and you've solved 80% of the potential problems.

- ☞ Choose a Model that Fits Your Culture: There is no one-size-fits-all governance model. A centralized approach might work for a small company, but most large organizations will thrive with a Hybrid model that balances central enablement with federated execution.

- ☞ Automate, Automate, Automate: This is the key to making governance practical and scalable. Embed your standards into the tools your developers already use. Use linters, automated compatibility checks, and code generation to make compliance the path of least resistance.

Further Reading

- Team Topologies by Matthew Skelton and Manuel Pais: While not strictly about EDA, this book is essential reading for understanding how to structure your teams for success in a distributed systems world. The concepts of a Platform Team and enabling teams are central to a good hybrid governance model.

- Designing Event-Driven Systems by Ben Stopford: A fantastic and practical book from a Confluent engineer. It offers deep insights into the nuances of event design, schema evolution, and the long-term consequences of your architectural choices.

- The AsyncAPI Blog (asyncapi.com/blog): We frequently post articles and tutorials on practical topics, including how to use tools like Spectral for linting, how to set up code generation pipelines, and best practices for documenting your event-driven architecture.

Strategy 17

Fostering a Community of Practice

Of all the strategies in this book, this one is the most human. It's the one that transforms a technical project into a living, breathing part of your company's culture. An Event-Driven Architecture (EDA) is not just a set of tools and patterns; it's a way of thinking and building. But a new way of thinking doesn't spread through memos and mandates. It spreads from person to person, through shared struggles, collaborative breakthroughs, and the simple act of helping each other out. Without a community, your beautiful architecture is just a blueprint in a drawer. With a community, it's a city that builds itself.

You've done the hard work of getting the initial buy-in. You've defined your standards and maybe even delivered a successful pilot project. But now you're starting to see a worrying trend. The team that worked on the pilot is miles ahead, but other teams are either hesitant to start or are making the same beginner mistakes you thought you'd solved. You see one team in the finance department spending weeks figuring out how to correctly implement an idempotent consumer for processing payments, while a team in logistics solved the exact same problem six months ago using a library they built internally. They just never told anyone. Knowledge is trapped in silos, and instead of building on each other's work, your organization is paying to solve the same problems over and over again.

You are here if...

- You see different teams reinventing the wheel to solve the same EDA-related problems.
- Your new architectural standards are adopted inconsistently because there's no central place for guidance, best practices, or help.
- You feel like you're playing a game of "whack-a-mole," correcting the same design flaws in one code review after another across different teams.
- Your best engineers feel isolated, and you worry they might leave to find a more vibrant and collaborative tech culture elsewhere.
- You're watching the momentum from your initial push slow down, not because of technical roadblocks, but because of a lack of connection.

The core principle of this strategy is this: Your EDA initiative's long-term success depends not on the technology you choose, but on the community you build around it. A technical specification is static. A wiki page is passive. But a community is a dynamic, self-sustaining engine for knowledge sharing, innovation, and support. It's the network that turns your architectural diagrams into a shared reality. Mandates create compliance, but communities create ownership. When people feel like they are part of something—a group of peers tackling interesting problems together—they stop being passive adopters and become active builders and champions of the new architecture. Your job isn't just to design the system; it's to nurture the ecosystem of people who will bring it to life.

The Action Plan

Building a community from scratch can feel intimidating, but it doesn't have to be a grand, top-down initiative. The most vibrant communities often start small, with a few passionate people and a clear purpose. The goal is to create a gravitational pull, drawing people in by consistently providing value and making it easy and rewarding to participate. Here's how you can do it, step-by-step.

Tactic 1: Lay the Foundation with Shared Spaces

Before a community can thrive, it needs a place to gather. In a modern, often distributed company, this means creating digital spaces that are easy to access and purpose-built for collaboration. The goal is to remove as much friction as possible from the act of asking a question, sharing a discovery, or finding a piece of information. If people don't know where to go, they'll go nowhere, and your community will never get off the ground.

First, create a dedicated communication channel. This is the community's digital town square. A public channel in your company's chat tool (like Slack or Microsoft Teams), perhaps named #eda-community or #event-architects, is perfect. This is the place for real-time conversation, quick questions, and announcements. It's where someone can post, "Hey, I'm trying to model an event for customer profile updates, has anyone done this before?" and get an answer in minutes instead of days. It lowers the barrier to asking for help and makes knowledge visible and searchable. This channel is your community's pulse; keep it active and encourage open discussion.

Second, establish a central knowledge base. While a chat channel is great for transient conversations, you need a more permanent home for valuable information. This is your community's library. Use a tool like Confluence, Notion, or even a well-organized Git repository with Markdown files. This space will house:

- Best Practices and Patterns: Documented solutions for common problems. How should we handle event versioning? What's our standard for retry logic? What does a good event schema look like?
- "How-To" Guides and Tutorials: Practical, step-by-step instructions for common tasks. For example, "Getting Started with RabbitMQ," "Creating Your First Event Consumer in Python," or "Using the Schema Registry."
- Decision Records: A log of important architectural decisions, explaining not just what was decided but why. This is incredibly valuable for new hires and provides context for your standards.
- A Catalog of Events: A discoverable, well-documented catalog of all the events in your system, what they mean, who produces them, and who consumes them. This is where tools like AsyncAPI and EventCatalog become absolutely critical for making your event landscape understandable and navigable.

Third, create a repository for shared assets. Don't just write about best practices; give people the code that implements them. A shared repository (e.g., in GitHub or GitLab) can host reusable code libraries, project templates (cookiecutter, dotnet new, or generated via the AsyncAPI CLI), and CI/CD pipeline configurations. This is the ultimate way to make the right way the easy way. When a developer can start a new event-driven service with a single command that automatically includes proper logging, metrics, and consumer logic, you've removed a huge amount of friction and ensured consistency.

These three spaces—the town square, the library, and the workshop—form the foundational infrastructure for your community.

Tactic 2: Create a Rhythm with Regular Events

Shared spaces are necessary, but they aren't sufficient. A library full of books is useless if no one ever visits. You need to create a regular cadence of events that brings people together, gives them a reason to engage, and keeps the momentum going. This rhythm is what makes the community feel alive and active.

Start with a monthly or bi-weekly Community of Practice (CoP) meeting. Keep it informal and focused on sharing. This isn't a status update meeting for management. It's a "show and tell" for practitioners. The format can be simple: two or three 15-minute slots where different teams or individuals share what they've been working on.

- "We just launched a new service that uses event sourcing. Here's what the architecture looks like and what we learned."
- "We were struggling with message ordering from our broker, and here's the clever solution we came up with."
- "I've been exploring the new features in Google Cloud Pub/Sub, and here's a demo of something cool you can do."

These sessions demystify the work being done across the company, spark new ideas, and create personal connections. Someone in the audience might see a presentation and realize it solves a problem they've been stuck on for weeks.

Next, organize hands-on workshops or learning dojos. While CoP meetings are for sharing, workshops are for doing. These are focused, practical sessions where participants actively code and learn a specific skill. Pick a single, concrete topic: "Building a Resilient Consumer with a Dead-Letter Queue," "Contract Testing for Events with AsyncAPI," or "Performance Tuning Your Message Broker." A senior engineer can lead the session, walking a group of 5-10 people through a pre-built exercise. This is an incredibly effective way to level up skills across the organization and ensure that your architectural patterns are not just understood but can be implemented correctly.

Consider hosting slightly more formal internal tech talks. These are less about a specific project and more about a broader topic. You could invite an experienced architect to give an "Introduction to Domain-Driven Design and EDA" or have a security expert explain "Best Practices for Securing Event Streams." These talks help build a shared vocabulary and understanding of the foundational concepts behind your architecture. Record these sessions and put them in your knowledge base for anyone who couldn't attend.

Finally, for a huge boost of energy and innovation, run an internal hackathon. Give teams a day or two to build something new and exciting using your event-driven platform. The theme could be broad ("Improve the Customer Experience") or specific ("Build a New Real-Time Analytics Dashboard"). Hackathons are amazing for generating enthusiasm, fostering cross-team collaboration, and quickly prototyping ideas that might turn into real products. The tangible output is great, but the real value is in the excitement and relationships built along the way.

Tactic 3: Fuel Participation by Making it Easy and Rewarding

You can have the best spaces and the most well-planned events, but if no one shows up or contributes, the community will fizzle out. You need to actively encourage participation by lowering the barrier to entry and making it clear that contributions are valued. People are busy, so you need to answer their unspoken question: "What's in it for me?"

First, make contributing easy. The path to sharing should be paved and well-lit.

- Use templates: Create simple templates for tech talk presentations or CoP "show and tell" slides. This removes the "blank page" problem and makes it less intimidating for someone to prepare.
- Have a clear process: Create a simple form or a tagged post in your chat channel for people to propose topics for meetings. Have a backlog of topics that you can pull from, so you're not scrambling for speakers before every meeting.
- Actively invite people: Don't just wait for volunteers. If you hear about a team doing something cool, reach out to them directly. Say, "Hey, I heard your team built a neat fraud detection service. It sounds awesome. Would you be willing to share a quick 15-minute overview at our next CoP meeting? The other teams would get a lot of value out of it." A personal invitation is much more effective than a general call for speakers.

Second, make contributing rewarding. Recognition is a powerful motivator. People want to feel that their efforts are seen and appreciated.

- Publicly praise contributors: When someone gives a great talk, shares a helpful code snippet, or answers a tough question in the chat, give them a public shout-out. A simple "@-mention" in the main channel saying, "Huge thanks to Sarah for that amazing deep dive on event versioning today!" goes a long way.

- Connect participation to growth: Work with engineering managers to formally recognize community contributions. If an engineer is mentoring others, improving shared libraries, or regularly sharing knowledge, that should be a positive data point in their performance review. It signals that the organization values "community work" as "real work."
- Create a "Wall of Fame": In your wiki, keep a running list of everyone who has presented at a CoP meeting or led a workshop. It's a small thing, but it creates a sense of history and acknowledges the people who have built the community.

By making it both easy and rewarding, you create a virtuous cycle: more people contribute, which increases the value of the community, which in turn attracts more people.

Tactic 4: Empower Champions and Distribute Ownership

A community that relies on a single person is fragile. If you, the initial advocate, get busy or move to a new role, the whole thing could collapse. To make the community sustainable, you must systematically distribute ownership and empower others to lead. Your goal is to evolve from being the community's leader to being its gardener.

Start by identifying potential champions. As your community grows, you'll notice people who are consistently active. They're the ones always answering questions in the chat, asking insightful questions in meetings, or showing genuine enthusiasm for the technology. These are your future leaders.

Once you've identified them, give them specific, manageable responsibilities. This is the key to avoiding burnout and making leadership feel accessible. Don't ask someone to "run the community." Instead, ask them to own a small, well-defined piece of it.

- "Hey Alex, you're always great at facilitating discussions. Would you be interested in being the official host for our monthly CoP meeting?"
- "Maria, your documentation is always super clear. Would you be willing to be the curator for our 'Best Practices' section in the wiki?"
- "Ben, you built that awesome project template. Would you be interested in being the official owner of our shared assets repository?"

This approach has several benefits. It reduces the workload on any one person. It gives people a sense of ownership and pride. And it builds resilience into the community—if the meeting host is on vacation, someone else can step in. Over time, you can form a small "steering committee" of these champions to guide the community's direction.

By empowering champions and distributing the work, you transform the community from "your project" into "our community." This is the final and most important step in ensuring that it will not only survive but thrive long after your initial push is over.

Story Time

This is a story from Jonas Lagoni, Senior Software Engineer, AsyncAPI TSC Member, and one of the first AsyncAPI contributors.

I learned this lesson the hard way while working on an open source code generation tool what it means to be a bottleneck and not share the responsibility across a community. As the main maintainer, I was drowning trying to review Python pull requests in the morning, debug Go issues at lunch, help with TypeScript questions in the evening, and somehow find time to work on the core architecture. Each language had its own quirks, idioms, and best practices that I was constantly trying to keep up with.

The breaking point came when I realized I was becoming the bottleneck. Contributors would submit a well-intentioned PR to fix a Java code generation bug, but I'd take a week to review it because I was buried in C# issues. Meanwhile, someone else would open an issue about the same Java problem, unaware that a fix was already waiting in my review queue. Talented contributors started walking away, frustrated by the slow feedback loop. I was watching passionate people lose interest simply because I couldn't keep up.

The transformation came when we shifted from a centralized model to a champion-based community. Instead of me trying to be the expert in everything, I identified passionate contributors who became "language champions" for Python, Go, TypeScript, and so on. I also created "input champions" for AsyncAPI and OpenAPI processing, and "core champions" for the underlying architecture. Each champion having complete autonomy over their domain.

The results were remarkable. Not only did response times improve dramatically, but the quality of solutions actually got better. The Python champion understood Python idioms far better than I did and could spot potential issues I would have missed. The Go champion knew the nuances of Go modules and could guide contributors toward more idiomatic solutions. Instead of one overloaded generalist, we had multiple focused experts who were genuinely excited about their specific areas.

Most importantly, contributors felt connected to real experts who understood their context. When someone had a TypeScript question, they weren't talking to someone who "kind of knew TypeScript"—they were talking to the TypeScript champion who lived and breathed it every day. The community became self-sustaining because champions took pride in their domains and actively sought out ways to improve them.

We made sure to recognize every contribution, no matter how small - bug reports, testing, documentation improvements, code contributions. But we especially celebrated our champions, because they were the foundation that made everything else possible. They transformed a one-person project into a thriving community where knowledge flowed freely and problems got solved quickly.

The 48-hour rule is crucial in open source where people contribute in their spare time, but the principle applies just as much in corporate environments. Think about a time when you were excited about contributing to something—when were you most motivated to continue? When you got quick, thoughtful feedback, or when your contribution disappeared into a black hole for weeks?

Common Pitfalls

- × Forcing Participation. The moment you make attendance at a CoP meeting mandatory, you kill the spirit. A community is a voluntary association of people who find value in it. Forced compliance breeds resentment, not engagement. Keep it optional and focus on making the content so good that people want to be there.

- × Letting it Become a Gripe Session. It's easy for a community forum to devolve into a place where people only complain about legacy systems, technical debt, or organizational problems. While venting has its place, a CoP must be relentlessly focused on constructive solutions. As a facilitator, your job is to steer the conversation from "This is broken" to "How can we work together to fix this?"

- × Lacking Management Support. The most common reason a CoP dies is that its members are not given the time to participate. If engineering managers view community activities as "a distraction from real work," it will fail. You must advocate for the CoP to leadership, framing it as a strategic investment in upskilling, efficiency, and retention. Show them the solved problems and the avoided rework.

× Ignoring the Beginners. It's natural for a community to become dominated by the voices of senior experts. Be intentional about creating a safe space for junior developers and people new to EDA. Host "beginner-friendly" sessions, encourage "stupid questions" (which are never stupid), and celebrate the progress of those just starting their journey.

Key Takeaways

☞ A Community is a Strategic Asset, Not a Nice-to-Have. Stop thinking of your job as just designing the architecture. Your primary role is to build the self-sustaining community of people who will bring it to life, maintain it, and evolve it. Mandates don't scale; communities do.

☞ Start Small and Build Momentum. Don't try to launch a massive, multi-faceted community program overnight. Start with one thing: a chat channel or a single show-and-tell meeting. Deliver value, generate a small win, and then build on that success, even if growth isn't linear.

☞ Make Connection the Path of Least Resistance. Create obvious, accessible digital spaces (chat, wiki, code repos) where people can connect and share. Remove every possible piece of friction between having a question and getting an answer from a peer.

☞ Recognize and Empower Others to Lead. Your goal is to make yourself redundant. Actively identify passionate champions and give them ownership of small, concrete parts of the community. A distributed leadership model is a resilient leadership model.

Further Reading

🕮 Cultivating Communities of Practice: A Guide to Managing Knowledge by Etienne Wenger, Richard McDermott, and William M. Snyder. This is the foundational book on the topic. It provides the theory and practice behind what makes communities of practice work.

🕮 The Art of Community: Seven Principles for Belonging by Charles H. Vogl. While not strictly a tech book, this provides incredible insight into the human dynamics of building strong, resilient communities. It's about creating a space where people feel they truly belong.

Strategy 18

Demonstrating Ongoing Value

You've done it. You championed the cause, you picked the right pilot project, you navigated the politics, and you launched your first service powered by an Event-Driven Architecture (EDA). The deployment was a success. The team celebrated, stakeholders were impressed, and for a moment, you were the hero. The champagne corks popped, the congratulatory emails were sent, and the initial excitement was palpable.

But a few months have passed. The buzz has faded. The "special project" is now just part of the production landscape. And the questions have started to change. They've shifted from "Can we do this?" to "Was it worth it?". And more importantly, "Should we do more of this?". The momentum you worked so hard to build is at risk of stalling. You know in your gut that the new system is better—it's faster, more resilient, and the developers who work on it are happier. But "gut feelings" don't secure budget for the next phase. You're standing at a critical juncture, where the future of EDA in your organization depends not on the success of the last launch, but on your ability to prove its ongoing, undeniable value.

You are here if...

- You feel like you've won the battle but might be losing the war.
- You delivered the pilot, but now you're struggling to articulate its long-term benefits in a way that resonates with business leaders.

- You lack the hard data to justify expanding the initiative, and you can feel the organization's attention drifting to the next "shiny object."
- You need a way to turn your initial success into a sustainable, strategic shift, but you're not sure how to keep the story alive and compelling.

The core principle of this strategy is this: A successful launch is not the finish line; it's the starting line for proving value. You must immediately shift from a project mindset ("we built the thing") to a product mindset ("we are continuously delivering value with the thing we built"). Your event-driven architecture isn't just a piece of technology; it's a value-generating product for your company. Like any product, it requires continuous measurement, iteration, and communication to demonstrate its worth and guide its evolution. Without this, your first success will become an isolated anecdote rather than the foundation of a transformation.

The Action Plan

To transition from a one-time win to a sustainable strategy, you need a systematic approach to demonstrating value. It's about making the benefits of EDA visible, tangible, and undeniable to everyone, from the engineers in the trenches to the executives in the boardroom.

Tactic 1: Build Your "Value Dashboard"

You can't prove value you can't measure. Your first and most critical task is to define what "better" actually looks like in concrete numbers. A common mistake is to only track technical metrics. While important, they don't tell the whole story and often mean nothing to business leaders. A robust Value Dashboard must translate technical improvements into business and even cultural outcomes. You should categorize your Key Performance Indicators (KPIs) into three distinct buckets.

- Technical KPIs: These are for you and your engineering teams. They measure the health and efficiency of your systems. These are the classic DORA metrics and other operational health indicators.
    - Lead Time for Changes: How long does it take from a code commit to that code successfully running in production? A key indicator of development velocity.
    - Deployment Frequency: How often do you release to production? EDA should enable more frequent, less risky deployments.

    - Mean Time To Recovery (MTTR): When a failure occurs, how quickly can you restore service? Loose-coupling in EDA often means failures are isolated and faster to fix.
    - Change Failure Rate: What percentage of deployments cause a failure in production? Smaller, independent services should lower this rate.
    - System Reliability/Error Rates: Track error rates for specific services. Are the new event-driven services more reliable under load than the old monolith components they replaced?
- Business KPIs: This is the most important bucket for securing future investment. This is where you translate the technical KPIs into the language of the business: money, time, and risk. You must work with product managers and business analysts to define these.
    - Time-to-Market for New Features: Use your "Lead Time" metric to show this. "We can now launch a new pricing rule in 2 days instead of 2 months because we don't have to redeploy the entire billing monolith."
    - Reduced Operational Costs: Did your new real-time processing system eliminate the need for expensive, oversized servers that ran nightly batch jobs? Quantify the savings in compute costs.
    - Increased Revenue/Recovered Sales: If your new event-driven inventory system provides real-time stock levels, you can calculate the reduction in "out-of-stock" errors that led to lost sales.
    - Improved Customer Satisfaction (CSAT): Can you correlate a drop in support tickets or an increase in CSAT scores with the rollout of a more responsive, reliable feature powered by EDA?
    - New Business Capabilities: Did your EDA platform enable a new product offering that wasn't possible before? For instance, "We can now offer real-time fraud alerts to our customers, a feature our competitors lack."
- Cultural KPIs: These are harder to quantify but are powerful indicators of a healthy engineering organization. They measure the impact on the people who have to build and maintain your systems.
    - Developer Satisfaction/Cognitive Load: Use simple surveys. Ask questions like, "On a scale of 1-10, how easy is it to build and ship a new feature in this domain?" A rising score is a huge win.
    - Team Autonomy: How many teams can deploy their services to production without coordinating with or waiting for other teams? This is a direct measure of how well you've achieved loose-coupling.

- Reduced Cross-Team Meetings: Can you show a reduction in the number of hours spent in planning and dependency-management meetings because teams can now work more independently? This is time given back to developers to actually write code.

Tactic 2: Automate Your Data Collection

Manually gathering metrics every week or month is a recipe for failure. It's tedious, error-prone, and it won't last. The moment you get busy, the reporting will slip, and your value story will disappear. You must make data collection an automated, integrated part of your systems.

This is not about buying a fancy new tool. It's about using what you already have.

- Leverage Observability and APM Tools: Instruments like Prometheus, Grafana, Datadog, or New Relic are perfect for tracking technical KPIs. You can create dashboards for MTTR, error rates, and system latency. Your CI/CD system (like Jenkins, GitLab CI, or CircleCI) is the source of truth for deployment frequency and lead time.
- Instrument for Business Events: To track business KPIs, you may need to add some instrumentation to your code. When a sale is processed, emit a SaleCompleted event with the order value. When an inventory update prevents an out-of-stock error, emit a StockSavedSale event. These business-level events can be fed into analytics platforms or even a simple message broker like RabbitMQ or Google Cloud Pub/Sub, allowing business analysts to build their own real-time dashboards.
- Integrate with Business Systems: Work with other departments. Can you get a data feed from the finance department's software to track cost savings? Can you get data from the customer support team's ticketing system (like Zendesk or Jira Service Management) to correlate deployments with ticket volume?

The goal is to make your Value Dashboard a living, breathing entity that requires zero manual effort to update. It should be the undeniable source of truth for the impact of your architecture.

Tactic 3: Create Stakeholder-Specific Narratives

Never send the same report to everyone. A CEO and a junior engineer care about vastly different things. Sending a deeply technical dashboard to a business executive is a waste of their time and makes you look like you don't understand what matters to them. You must tailor your communication to the audience.

- For the Executive Team (The "One-Pager"): They need a high-level, quarterly summary that fits on a single page or slide. Focus exclusively on business KPIs. Use visuals and focus on trends.
- Bad: "We reduced P99 latency for the user-profile-service by 200ms and increased deployment frequency by 50%."
- Good: "This quarter, our architectural improvements allowed us to launch the new partner integrations 4 weeks ahead of schedule, directly contributing to our Q3 revenue goals. Furthermore, we've reduced customer-facing errors during peak traffic by 60%, protecting the brand experience."
- For Product and Engineering Leadership (The "Trend Report"): These leaders sit at the intersection of technology and business. Provide them with a more detailed monthly report. Show them the technical KPI trends (like cycle time and MTTR) and directly connect them to the business KPIs (like time-to-market and CSAT scores). This helps them justify their headcount and budget, and it shows them that your platform is making their teams' lives better.
- For Development Teams (The "Real-Time Dashboard"): Give this to them on a screen they can see every day. They should see their deployment frequency, their service's error rates, and the lead time for their changes in real-time. This creates a tight feedback loop. When they see a change they just pushed cause the error rate to spike, they can react immediately. It connects their daily work to tangible outcomes and empowers them to take ownership of their service's quality.

Tactic 4: Host a Quarterly "Value Review"

Emailing reports is passive. To truly drive the message home, you need to actively narrate the story behind the data. Schedule a recurring 45-minute meeting every quarter with key stakeholders: business leaders, product managers, and engineering managers. Don't call it a "Tech Review"; call it the "Business Value & Technology Roadmap" meeting or something similar.

Use this session to:

- Celebrate the Wins: Briefly present the highlights from your Value Dashboard. "As you can see, our ability to experiment with pricing has increased by 400% this quarter, thanks to the new event-driven promotion engine."

- Be Transparent About Challenges: Share where things aren't going as well. "While our reliability is up, the data shows that onboarding a new developer to this new way of working is still taking too long. This is a problem we need to solve." This builds incredible trust.
- Use Data to Propose What's Next: This is the most crucial part. You use the data from your dashboard to justify the next strategic investment. "We've proven we can improve time-to-market for customer-facing features. The data from our CI/CD system, however, shows that the biggest bottleneck remaining is our legacy data warehouse batch processing. We propose our next initiative should be to create a real-time data streaming pipeline, and we project this will unlock real-time personalization, which Product has wanted for two years."

This meeting transforms you from a technology provider into a strategic partner. You are no longer just asking for money; you are presenting a data-backed business case for how the company can win.

Story Time

The following is a story from Samir Amzani, API Strategist and Co-Author of the book RESTful API Design Patterns and Best Practices.

Here's the thing nobody tells you about API transformations: the hardest part isn't building the technology. It's proving why it matters after you've built it.

I learned this the hard way during our API vision rollout at Back Market. We'd spent months crafting what we thought was a brilliant strategy: API discovery, consistency, developer experience, the whole nine yards. We had 30 stream-aligned teams, an API enablement squad, champions embedded in every corner of the organization. From a technical standpoint, we were crushing it.

But then came the quarterly review that almost ended everything.

Our VP of Engineering, had been getting pressure from leadership about our API investments. The industry stats were scary: API work was costing companies around 60 billion USD globally. That's iPhone 14 Pro money, massive carbon footprints, the works. And here we were, asking for more budget to expand our API program.

"Samir," our VP said, pulling up a spreadsheet that made my stomach drop, "we need to talk about the elephant in the room. Our API chapter has been running for eight months now. We've got tooling, we've got processes, we've got champions.

But what do we actually have to show for it?"

The spreadsheet was brutal. Dozens of APIs across our platform, each one consuming engineering time, infrastructure costs, maintenance overhead. From the outside, it looked like we were just creating expensive complexity.

Here's where I almost lost the whole program. I started rattling off the usual suspects: "We've improved consistency! Our Spectral linting catches more errors! Our developer portal usage is up!"

Our VP just stared at me. "That's great, but what does that mean for the business? Are we shipping features faster? Are we reducing support tickets? Are we making more money?"

I had no idea.

That was my wake-up call. We'd been so focused on building the perfect API governance machine that we'd forgotten to measure whether it was actually working for the people who mattered: our engineers, our customers, our business.

Instead of trying to defend what we'd built, I took a step back. We needed to understand what was actually broken and measure it properly. That's when we identified our three categories of urgency:

API Discovery Urgency: Our SRE team was spending hours tracking down which API was causing incidents. Mean Time To Recovery was through the roof because engineers couldn't quickly find the right service owner or understand API dependencies.

API Consistency Urgency: Every team was building APIs differently. Some used REST, others went with GraphQL, most just did whatever felt right. Integration between teams was becoming a nightmare.

API Experience Urgency: Our frontend teams were constantly frustrated. They'd spend days just figuring out how to authenticate with a backend service, let alone actually use it.

But here's the key: we started measuring these problems in business terms, not just engineering complaints.

Working with our data team, we started tracking what actually moved the needle:

- Developer Productivity: How long does it take an engineer to find and integrate with an API they need? We went from engineers spending 2-3 days per integration to finding APIs in under 5 minutes. That's not just a nice-to-have, that's dozens of engineering hours saved per week.

- Incident Response: Our MTTR for API-related incidents dropped by 60% because engineers could actually find the right service owners and understand dependencies through our centralized API portal.
- Feature Velocity: This was the big one. Teams using our standardized API tooling were shipping features 40% faster than teams still doing their own thing. Why? Because they weren't reinventing authentication, error handling, and documentation every single time.

But the metric that really got leadership's attention was our API Consumer NPS. We'd gone from -15 (engineers actively hated working with internal APIs) to +10 in just six months.

The quarterly review was make-or-break time. Instead of showing up with technical metrics, I focused on the human impact:

"Eight months ago, our engineers were spending 15% of their time just figuring out how to talk to each other's services. Today, 50% of our engineers can find and integrate with any API in under five minutes."

I showed them the NPS chart: that brutal swing from -15 to +10. "This isn't just about developer happiness. Happy engineers ship faster. Our teams using standardized API tooling are delivering features 40% faster than teams still doing their own thing."

Then came the slide that changed everything: "Cost of Not Having API Standards." We'd calculated that our old way of working was costing us about 3 full-time engineers worth of productivity per quarter, just in duplicated effort, debugging integration issues, and reinventing the same solutions over and over.

The room went quiet. Then the CTO leaned forward: "So you're telling me this API program is actually saving us money?"

"More than that," I said. "It's making us faster. And in the refurbished electronics business, faster means we get the best inventory before our competitors do."

Looking back, that API vision journey at Back Market taught me three things that I've carried into every API initiative since:

- Start with urgency, not technology. We didn't begin by building the perfect API gateway or the most elegant OpenAPI specs. We started by identifying the three pain points that were actually costing us money: discovery chaos, consistency nightmares, and developer experience friction. Only then did we build solutions.
- Make the invisible visible. Engineers knew our API landscape was messy, but leadership had no idea how messy until we put numbers on it. Going from 15% to 50% of engineers being able to find APIs quickly isn't just a nice metric. It's proof that we'd eliminated a massive hidden tax on productivity.

- Culture follows measurement. The real magic happened when we stopped pushing API standards and started proving their value. Once engineers could see that our tooling made their lives easier (NPS from -15 to +10), they started asking for more, not less, governance. The API champions went from being change agents to being internal consultants that teams actually wanted to work with.

What happened next was the real magic. Once leadership saw the numbers, everything changed. Our API enablement team went from being seen as "overhead" to being seen as "productivity multipliers."

We started getting requests from teams to help them adopt our standards. The API champions in each squad went from pushing changes uphill to being pulled into planning sessions. Engineers started contributing to our API guidelines because they could see how it made their own work easier.

Six months later, we published that blog post about our API vision. Not because marketing asked us to, but because other companies started reaching out, asking how we'd made API governance actually work.

Here's what I learned at Back Market: great API governance isn't about having the perfect OpenAPI specs or the most sophisticated tooling. It's about solving real problems that engineers face every day and being able to prove you've actually solved them.

The breakthrough wasn't technical. It was realizing that API governance is a people problem disguised as a technology problem. Once we started measuring developer happiness alongside system performance, everything else fell into place.

The technology we built was solid but not groundbreaking. What made the difference was shifting from "look at this cool thing we built" to "here's how this thing makes everyone more successful."

And that CTO who'd been questioning our budget? He became our biggest advocate, regularly citing our work as proof that "good engineering practices are business investments, not costs."

Common Pitfalls

× Tracking Vanity Metrics. Don't get caught up in metrics like "millions of events published per day" or "number of microservices." These numbers are meaningless without business context. A million events could be valuable, or they could just be noise flooding your system. Always ask, "Does this metric track a real business outcome?" If the answer is no, it's a vanity metric.

- × Forgetting the Baseline. If you don't measure the pain of the old system before you start, you can never prove the new system is better. Before you write a single line of code for your next EDA project, take a snapshot of the current state: What's the current time-to-market? What's the current error rate? What are the current operational costs? This baseline is your most powerful tool.
- × One-Size-Fits-All Reporting. The fastest way to get your report ignored is to send your detailed technical dashboard to your Head of Sales. It demonstrates that you don't understand or respect their world. Tailor the message, the format, and the language to each audience. Speak in terms of business value to business leaders and technical excellence to technical leaders.

Key Takeaways

- ☞ Shift from Project to Product. Your EDA initiative doesn't end at launch. You are now the owner of a value-generating product. Your job is to measure, communicate, and enhance that value over time.
- ☞ Build a Multi-Faceted Value Dashboard. Go beyond technical metrics. Create a balanced set of KPIs that cover the Technical (how efficient?), Business (how profitable?), and Cultural (how empowering?) impact of your work.
- ☞ Translate Technical Wins into Business Outcomes. This is the single most important skill for driving sustained architectural change. "Lower latency" is a technical win. "Fewer abandoned shopping carts" is a business outcome. Learn to make that translation fluently.
- ☞ Automate and Communicate Continuously. Make measurement an effortless, automated part of your process. Then, turn that data into compelling, audience-specific narratives to build unstoppable momentum for your initiative.

Further Reading

- 🕮 Accelerate: The Science of Lean Software and DevOps by Nicole Forsgren, Jez Humble, and Gene Kim. This is the definitive book on the DORA metrics (Lead Time, Deployment Frequency, MTTR, Change Failure Rate). It provides the research and evidence proving why these technical metrics are direct predictors of high-performing organizations.
- 🕮 Team Topologies: Organizing Business and Technology Teams for Fast Flow by Matthew Skelton and Manuel Pais. This book is essential for understanding and measuring the "cultural" KPIs. It provides a framework

for designing teams to minimize cognitive load and maximize autonomy—outcomes that EDA is perfectly suited to enable.

- 🕮 Measure What Matters by John Doerr. While focused on Objectives and Key Results (OKRs), this book is a masterclass in how to connect ambitious goals to concrete, measurable results. It will shape how you think about defining and tracking your business KPIs.

Cultural & Long-Term Strategies

Embedding the Shift Organization-Wide

Strategy 19

Enabling Organization-Wide Adoption

The chaos has subsided. Your organization has successfully navigated the turbulent early days of Event-Driven Architecture. You have a well-established Event Catalog that serves as the single source of truth. Teams have access to onboarding materials and starter kits, allowing them to build new event-driven services with a degree of confidence and consistency. You've won the war for adoption. But now you're facing a new, more subtle challenge: the long peace.

You see it when you review a new service design. The team used the catalog to find the right events, and their code connects to the broker perfectly, but their consumer logic is inefficient and brittle. You see it when another team, faced with a multi-step business process, reverts to a chain of synchronous API calls because they don't know how to orchestrate a long-running saga with events. Your people know the basic moves, but they haven't mastered the craft. The initial success has led to a plateau of competence, and the gap between your most and least skilled teams is widening.

You are here if...

- You have great tools, but teams are still making beginner mistakes in their architectural design.

- Your onboarding documents show people how to produce an event, but not why they should design their consumers for idempotency.
- The same small group of "EDA gurus" are still the only ones who can solve complex asynchronous problems, creating a persistent bottleneck for innovation.
- Your organization is good at EDA, but you know it needs to become great.

The core principle of this strategy that you must now embrace is this: Tools provide consistency, but only people create excellence. Your challenge has evolved beyond enabling adoption; you must now actively cultivate mastery. To truly scale your architecture's potential, you have to scale the deep expertise of the people who build it. It's time to stop just giving them a map and start teaching them how to be world-class navigators.

The Action Plan

Moving an entire organization from competence to mastery is not a passive process. It requires a deliberate, multi-faceted strategy to deepen knowledge, formalize learning, and create a self-perpetuating culture of expertise. You already have the foundation; now it's time to build a world-class training academy on top of it.

Tactic 1: Evolve Onboarding Docs into a Learning Ecosystem

Your existing onboarding materials are good for getting people started, but they are a static resource. To drive mastery, you need to transform them from a simple "getting started" guide into a living, interactive learning ecosystem that helps engineers solve real-world problems.

- Create "The EDA Cookbook": Go beyond the "Hello, World!" example. Build a collection of practical, opinionated "recipes" that provide solutions to common, advanced challenges your teams face. This cookbook should be a central part of your developer portal. Example recipes could include:
    - "Recipe: Implementing the Saga Pattern for a Multi-Step Booking Process"
    - "Recipe: Ensuring Idempotency with a Message ID Cache"
    - "Recipe: Handling Out-of-Order Events in an Analytics Pipeline"
    - "Recipe: Graceful Degradation When a Downstream System is Slow"
    - Each recipe should include not just code snippets, but also the design rationale, trade-offs, and links to real examples within your company.

- Introduce Interactive Sandboxes: Reading about a pattern is one thing; building it is another. Integrate hands-on, self-service learning tools (like Killercoda, or build your own) that provide a safe sandbox environment. Let engineers experiment with, break, and fix complex event-driven flows without any risk to production systems. A one-hour interactive tutorial on debugging a failing saga is worth more than a ten-page document.
- Build In a Feedback Loop: Your documentation should not be a monologue. On every page of your cookbook and your guides, add a simple mechanism for feedback—a "Was this page helpful?" widget or a link to "Suggest an improvement in Slack." Actively monitor this feedback and use it to constantly iterate and improve your materials. This turns your entire engineering organization into a content improvement team.

Tactic 2: Launch a Tiered Training and Certification Program

Workshops are good, but a structured curriculum is better. To systematically raise the skill level across the board, develop a formal, internal training program with clear levels of proficiency. This creates a visible path for career growth and gamifies the learning process.

- Level 1: The "EDA Driver's License": This is the mandatory baseline for any engineer joining a team that builds or maintains event-driven systems. It's a short, focused course covering the essentials: how to use the event catalog, your company's core design principles, how to interpret SLOs for event streams, and the basics of observability. Passing this demonstrates fundamental competence.
- Level 2: The "Advanced Patterns" Course: This is an optional but highly encouraged track for mid-level and senior engineers. It's a deep dive into the complex topics that separate the competent from the expert: choreography vs. orchestration, saga implementation patterns, event sourcing, and strategies for testing asynchronous systems.
- Level 3: The "Architect's Masterclass": This is an exclusive, cohort-based program for your most senior engineers and architects. The focus here is less on implementation and more on strategy: applying Domain-Driven Design to a complex event-driven landscape, managing socio-technical boundaries between teams, and planning the long-term evolution of your event platform.

To add weight to this program, create a simple internal "certification" for each level. An "EDA Certified Practitioner" badge on an internal profile is a powerful motivator and makes expertise visible within the organization.

Tactic 3: Formalize a Mentorship and Coaching Network

The most effective learning often happens peer-to-peer. You need to formalize a system that allows your experts to transfer their knowledge through direct, hands-on coaching, not just by answering questions in a chat channel.

- Establish "EDA Dojos": A "Dojo" is an immersive coaching engagement. It's not a meeting; it's a temporary assignment. When a team is about to start a major new event-driven project, an expert (a "sensei") is embedded with them for two to four weeks. They don't write the code for the team; they pair-program, lead design sessions, and coach them through the difficult decisions. This is the single most effective way to transmit deep, tacit knowledge.

- Empower a "Champions" Program: You can't scale if your few central experts are the only mentors. Identify and empower EDA "Champions"—passionate experts located within different business domains and product teams. Give these Champions official recognition, a budget of "mentoring time" each quarter, and a direct line to the core platform team. They become the local, trusted advisors, scaling your coaching capabilities immensely.

- Run Collaborative Design Reviews: Ditch the intimidating, formal architecture review board. Instead, have your Champions host open "Office Hours" or "Whiteboarding Sessions." Teams can voluntarily bring their designs for a collaborative, low-stakes discussion. The goal is to coach and improve the design together, not to pass or fail it.

Tactic 4: Amplify Knowledge Through Evangelism and Shared Learning

You need to create a constant, low-level hum of learning throughout the organization. This means proactively sharing knowledge, celebrating successes, and, most importantly, learning from failures.

- Go on a Roadshow: Don't just wait for people to come to your monthly "EDA Guild" meeting. Take the knowledge to them. Proactively schedule 30-minute slots in team-level meetings to showcase a new Cookbook recipe, demo a successfully launched project, or share a key learning.

- Normalize Blameless Post-Mortems: When an incident occurs in your event-driven systems, it is a precious learning opportunity. Write a detailed, blameless post-mortem that focuses on the systemic causes, not individual mistakes. Share this document widely. The lessons from one team's painful outage can prevent ten other teams from falling into the same trap.

- Host "Failure Fridays": Create a safe space for engineers to share stories of things that went wrong. An engineer presenting on "How my misunderstanding of at-least-once delivery caused duplicate notifications" is one of the most powerful and memorable training sessions you can possibly run.

Common Pitfalls

× The Expert's Curse. When your top experts create training materials, they often forget what it's like not to know everything. They create content that is technically accurate but too dense and abstract for someone still learning. All materials must be reviewed by recent learners.

× Training for Training's Sake. Hosting a workshop on a cool, emerging technology that has no immediate application to your company's problems. All training must be grounded in your specific tech stack, your patterns, and your business domain to be effective.

× Ignoring the Incentives. Asking your senior engineers to spend hours per week mentoring, coaching, and writing documentation without making it a formal part of their job description and performance review. If "community contribution" isn't rewarded, it will always be the first thing dropped when project deadlines loom.

Key Takeaways

☞ From Adoption to Mastery. The goal is no longer just to get people using EDA; it's to get them using it exceptionally well. Your focus must shift from providing access to cultivating expertise.

☞ Teach Recipes, Not Just Rules. Move beyond basic instructions. Provide your teams with a cookbook of practical, opinionated solutions to the complex, real-world problems they face every day.

☞ Coach Hands-On, Don't Just Advise from Afar. Deep expertise is best transferred through immersive, hands-on coaching. Use Dojos and embedded mentorship to accelerate learning in a way no document ever can.

☞ Amplify Every Lesson. Every success and, more importantly, every failure is a learning opportunity for the entire organization. Create channels to proactively share these lessons widely, ensuring that one team's experience benefits everyone.

Further Reading

- Apprenticeship Patterns: Guidance for the Aspiring Software Craftsman by Dave Hoover and Adewale Oshineye. While about software craftsmanship in general, its patterns for mentorship, learning, and skill progression are perfectly applicable to building an internal EDA academy.
- The Field Guide to Understanding 'Human Error' by Sidney Dekker. If you want to build a truly effective culture of blameless post-mortems and shared learning from failure, this book is the essential starting point. It will change how you think about incidents.
- Drive: The Surprising Truth About What Motivates Us by Daniel Pink. As you design your training and mentorship programs, understanding the core human motivators—Autonomy, Mastery, and Purpose—will help you create a system that people are genuinely excited to participate in.

Strategy 20

Amplifying Success Stories

Imagine this: Deep in the digital engine room of your company, a small team of engineers has just pulled off something amazing. They replaced a clunky, monolithic service that caused constant production fires with a sleek, event-driven solution. For the first time in years, their on-call rotations are quiet. They can ship new features in days instead of weeks. It's a huge win. They celebrate with a team lunch, write a few lines in their sprint-end report, and move on to the next ticket. Six months later, you look around the organization and realize a frustrating truth: nothing has changed. That pocket of excellence remains just that—a pocket. Nobody else knows about their success, nobody has learned from it, and the rest of the company is still fighting the same old fires. The victory was real, but its impact died on the vine.

You are here if...

- You've delivered a successful Event-Driven Architecture pilot, but it feels like a tree falling in an empty forest.
- Your team has clear proof that this new way of working is better, but you're struggling to get other teams to even notice, let alone adopt it.
- You might feel like you're constantly having to re-justify the value of EDA, even when the evidence is right in front of you.

- You've won the battle, but you're not sure how to leverage that victory to win the larger war for architectural transformation.

The core principle of this strategy is this: Success that isn't shared is a failure of imagination. A successful project that goes uncelebrated is a wasted opportunity. Your job as an advocate for change extends beyond the code and the architecture diagrams. You must also become the chief storyteller and internal marketer for your cause. Building a great system is only half the job; the other half is building a powerful, compelling narrative around it that inspires others to follow your lead. Without this, even the most brilliant technical achievements remain isolated triumphs instead of catalysts for broad, organizational change.

The Action Plan

To turn isolated wins into a wave of adoption, you need a deliberate plan to find, frame, and broadcast your success stories. It's not about bragging; it's about providing a blueprint for others. This is internal marketing, and when done right, it's one of the most powerful tools you have.

Tactic 1: Become a Success Detective

You can't share stories you don't know exist. Your first job is to actively hunt for them. Don't wait for people to volunteer their wins; they're often too busy or too humble. You need to become a detective, actively seeking out the evidence that EDA is working.

Start by defining what "success" even means in your context. It's not a single thing. Create a checklist of potential wins to look for, covering multiple dimensions:

- Technical & Operational Metrics: These are the hard numbers. Look for things like reduced system latency, lower error rates, decreased server costs, or improved system uptime. A huge one is the reduction in mean time to recovery (MTTR) after an incident. Event-driven systems can often isolate failures, making recovery much faster.
- Developer Experience Metrics: This is about making engineers' lives better. Are teams shipping code faster? Is the onboarding time for new developers shorter because they only need to understand a small, loosely-coupled service? Talk to the teams. Ask them: "How has this changed your day-to-day work?" A reduction in on-call alerts or pages is a massive quality-of-life improvement that resonates with every engineer.

- Business & Product Metrics: This is the language that gets leaders excited. Did the new system enable a feature that was previously impossible? Has it reduced customer churn because of a more reliable service? Did it decrease the time to process a customer order, leading to higher satisfaction? Connect the technical win to a tangible business outcome. For example, a real-time inventory system isn't just a cool tech project; it's a tool that prevents stockouts and lost sales.

- Qualitative & Human Impact: Don't underestimate the power of human stories. A quote from a product manager saying, "We can finally experiment with new features without fear of breaking the whole system," is incredibly powerful. A developer admitting, "I don't dread being on-call anymore," is a story that will spread like wildfire among their peers.

Systematically gather this data. Set up short, informal interviews with teams who have implemented an event-driven service. Look at their dashboards. Read their retrospectives. Your goal is to build a case file for each success story, backed by both data and human experience.

Tactic 2: Craft the Story, Not Just the Report

Once you have the raw data, you need to shape it into a narrative. People don't remember spreadsheets; they remember stories. A dry report stating "Service X reduced latency by 150ms" is forgettable. A story about how that latency reduction saved the customer support team from angry calls during a peak sales event is memorable.

Use the classic story structure:

- The Setting & The Hero: Introduce the team. Who are they? What part of the business do they support? Make them relatable. The hero isn't the technology; it's the team that wielded it.

- The Villain & The Conflict: Describe the problem in vivid terms. What was the "old way"? Was it a monstrous monolith? A tangled web of point-to-point integrations? A slow, unreliable batch process that everyone hated? Talk about the pain it caused—the late-night pages, the frustrated customers, the missed business opportunities.

- The Journey & The Discovery: Explain how the team decided to try EDA. What was their thought process? What were the challenges they faced during implementation? Being honest about the struggles makes the story more credible and provides valuable lessons for others.

- The Victory & The Resolution: This is where you bring in the results. Present the "before and after" using the metrics you gathered. "Before, it took us six weeks to add a new shipping partner. Now, with our new OrderFulfilled event, we can add one in two days." Follow up the hard data with the human impact. "The team now spends 80% of their time on new features instead of maintenance."

- The Moral of the Story: What is the key takeaway for the rest of the organization? It could be "Loose-coupling gives teams the autonomy to move faster," or "Thinking in events unlocks new business capabilities we never thought possible."

Package this story in different formats for different audiences. The core narrative remains the same, but the emphasis changes. For engineers, you might focus more on the technical details and developer experience wins. For product managers, you highlight the speed to market. For executives, you lead with the business outcomes and risk reduction.

Tactic 3: Go Multi-Channel with Your Message

If you only use one channel to share your story, you'll only reach one audience. To create a real organizational buzz, you need to become a master of internal communications, using every platform at your disposal.

- Internal Tech Blog/Wiki: This is your home base. Write a detailed post for each success story, complete with the full narrative, data, and maybe even some code snippets or architecture diagrams. This becomes the "source of truth" you can link to from other communications.

- Tech Talks & Lunch-and-Learns: This is the most effective format for peer-to-peer influence. Invite the team who built the system to present their work. A live demo is worth a thousand slides. Seeing their peers confidently explain how they solved a common problem is what convinces other engineers to try it themselves. Record these sessions and make them available on-demand.

- Company & Department Newsletters: Don't just talk to the tech people. Write a short, punchy summary of the success story for the company-wide newsletter. Focus on the business impact. An executive who reads, "The platform team's new architecture just cut our customer onboarding time in half," is more likely to approve your budget for the next EDA initiative.

- Short Video Clips: Record a two-minute interview with the product manager or tech lead from the successful team. Ask them three simple questions: What was the problem? What did you do? What was the result? Post it on your internal social channels like Slack or Microsoft Teams. These clips are easily digestible and highly shareable.

- Demos at All-Hands Meetings: Getting five minutes at a company or departmental all-hands meeting is gold. This is your chance to reach a broad audience that includes people from sales, marketing, and finance. Show, don't just tell. A quick demo of a real-time dashboard powered by events is far more impactful than a slide full of bullet points.

The key is to create a surround-sound effect. Someone might ignore the email newsletter, but then they see a message about it on Slack, and then a colleague mentions the tech talk. This repetition across multiple channels is what makes the message stick.

Tactic 4: Build a "Success Library"

One-off announcements are good, but their impact fades over time. To create lasting change, you need to build a permanent, accessible repository of your success stories. Think of it as your "EDA Hall of Fame" or "Success Library."

This should be a simple, easy-to-navigate space on your internal wiki or developer portal. For each success story, create a page that includes:

- A one-paragraph summary of the win.
- A link to the full blog post or case study.
- The recording of the tech talk or demo.
- Key metrics and business outcomes in a scannable format.
- Contact information or a link to the team's channel for anyone who wants to learn more.

This library becomes an invaluable asset. When a new engineer joins the company, you can point them to it as an example of "how we build things here." When a team is hesitant to adopt EDA, you can send them a link to a story of another team that solved a very similar problem. When you're making a budget request for new infrastructure or tooling, you can reference the library as proof of the ROI.

This centralized resource transforms your advocacy from a series of disconnected efforts into a structured, evidence-based campaign. It shows that EDA isn't just a theory; it's a proven, practical approach that delivers real results for your company.

Common Pitfalls

When you start amplifying your successes, it's easy to misstep. The goal is to inspire, not to alienate. Watch out for these common traps.

- × Forgetting the "Why" for the "What." Avoid getting bogged down in the technical implementation details when speaking to a broad audience. They don't care that you used a specific message broker or serialization format. They care about what it enabled. Instead of saying, "We implemented an idempotent consumer using a persistent message log," say, "We built a system that guarantees a customer is never billed twice, even if our service restarts."
- × Making it Sound Like an Ivory Tower Proclamation. The story should come from the team that did the work, not from an architecture group dictating from on high. Let the engineers be the heroes of their own story. When success is presented by peers, it feels authentic and achievable. When it's presented by management, it can feel like a mandate, which can trigger resistance.
- × Presenting a Perfect, Flawless Journey. If you only talk about the amazing results and gloss over the challenges, your story will lack credibility. Engineers, in particular, will be skeptical. Be open about the roadblocks you hit. Did you struggle with choosing a broker? Was it hard to get event schemas right? Sharing these struggles makes the success more real and provides invaluable lessons for the teams who will follow.

Key Takeaways

- ☞ Your Job Isn't Done at Deployment: The work of an EDA advocate isn't finished when the code is pushed to production. That's when the work of advocacy begins. You must shift your focus from building the system to broadcasting its success.
- ☞ Translate Wins into Every Language: A single success story contains multiple narratives. Learn to extract the right one for each audience. Talk about operational stability with engineers, speed-to-market with product managers, and business ROI with executives.
- ☞ Stories Move People, Data Justifies Decisions: Lead with a compelling story that frames the problem, the struggle, and the victory. Use the human element to create an emotional connection. Then, back up your story with the hard data and metrics that give it credibility.
- ☞ Create a System for Sharing: Don't rely on ad-hoc announcements. Be deliberate. Use a multi-channel approach (blogs, tech talks, newsletters) and

create a central, permanent "Success Library" that becomes the cornerstone of your advocacy efforts and a resource for the entire organization.

Further Reading

- Made to Stick: Why Some Ideas Survive and Others Die by Chip Heath & Dan Heath: This is the definitive guide to making your ideas memorable and shareable. Its principles on simplicity, concreteness, and storytelling are directly applicable to internal tech marketing.
- Show Your Work! by Austin Kleon: A short, inspiring book about the importance of sharing your process and your results. It will help you get over the fear of "bragging" and see sharing as an act of generosity.
- Internal Marketing: A New Perspective for Modern Management by Rafiq and Ahmed: While more academic, this provides a solid theoretical foundation for why internal marketing is critical for implementing any new strategy or cultural change within a company. It helps frame your efforts in a more strategic context.

Strategy 21

Cultivating Psychological Safety

An engineer on your team, Fatima, is staring at her screen. She's quiet. In the architecture review meeting, you've just finished whiteboarding the flow for a new critical service that will process payment authorization events. It's complex, involving multiple consumers, a saga pattern for rollbacks, and a new event schema you're particularly proud of. You ask, "Any questions? Concerns?" The room is silent. The senior engineers nod, already thinking about implementation. Fatima, who's only been with the company for six months, thinks she sees a potential race condition, a tiny window where a customer could be double-charged if two events arrive in a specific, unlikely order. But she stays quiet. The senior architect seems so confident. Everyone else seems to get it. She doesn't want to look stupid by asking a "what if" question that's probably nothing. She tells herself it's a long shot. No big deal.

Three months later, it is a very big deal. A marketing campaign creates an unexpected load pattern, the exact "long shot" scenario Fatima had worried about. For two hours, hundreds of high-value transactions are double-charged. The fallout is a nightmare: furious customers, a frantic all-hands-on-deck effort to fix the data, and a huge blow to the company's reputation. The post-mortem meeting is tense. Fingers are pointed. The question isn't "How did our system allow this to happen?" but "Whose code failed?" The trust within the team takes a nosedive. Fatima learns her lesson: keep your head down and your mouth shut.

You are here if…

- You feel a pit in your stomach when an incident alert fires, not because the system is down, but because you know the blame game is about to begin.
- Your team meetings are filled with silence and cautious agreement, even when you're discussing complex and risky architectural changes.
- Your engineers avoid experimenting with new patterns or technologies for fear of being the one whose name is attached to a failure.
- The phrase "we learn from our mistakes" is something people say, but what they really mean is "we find out who made the mistake and make sure it doesn't happen again."

The core principle of this strategy is this: Event-Driven Architecture is an exercise in managing distributed complexity, and you cannot manage that complexity without open, fearless communication. The single greatest enabler of that communication is psychological safety. It's the shared belief that the team is safe for interpersonal risk-taking. It means you can speak up with an idea, a question, or a concern—or admit a mistake—without fear of being shamed, blamed, or humiliated. Without this safety net, your team is flying blind. The small doubts, the critical observations, and the early warnings that could prevent catastrophic failures—like Fatima's—stay buried under a layer of fear. Building a resilient EDA is not just about resilient technology; it's about building a resilient team culture to match.

The Action Plan

Building a culture of psychological safety isn't about group hugs or avoiding tough conversations. It's about intentionally engineering your team's interactions so that candor is not just possible, but normal. It requires deliberate, consistent action from leaders and peers alike.

Tactic 1: Model Vulnerability First

Psychological safety starts at the top. As a leader, architect, or senior engineer, you have a disproportionate impact on your team's culture. Your team is watching you for cues on how to behave. If you project an aura of perfection and infallibility, you create a standard that no one can meet, forcing them to hide their own imperfections. The most powerful thing you can do is be the first to be vulnerable.

This means admitting when you don't know something. Instead of bluffing your way through a question about a new feature in AWS EventBridge, say, "That's a great question. I'm not actually sure how that new filtering mechanism works under the hood. Can someone help me understand it?" This simple act does two things: it shows that it's okay not to have all the answers, and it invites collaboration.

It also means owning your mistakes, publicly and without excuses. When a design decision you made turns out to be flawed, you need to be the one to say it. "I pushed for us to use a single event topic for all customer-related events, and now we're seeing that it's creating a messy web of dependencies for our consumers. That was my call, and it was the wrong one. Let's figure out a better approach together." When you do this, you're not showing weakness; you're showing strength. You are modeling that the goal is not to be right, but to get it right. You are giving your team permission to be human, to take risks, and to learn.

Tactic 2: Reframe Failure as Valuable Data

In a complex, loosely-coupled system, failure is inevitable. An event producer will ship a malformed payload. A consumer will have a bug that creates a poison pill message, blocking a whole queue. A broker configuration will be set incorrectly, causing messages to be dropped silently. These are not moral failings. They are data points about the brittleness of your system. Your response to these moments defines your culture.

To build psychological safety, you must surgically remove blame from your vocabulary and your thought process. Shift the language you use away from people and toward processes and systems.

- Instead of: "Who broke the deployment?"
- Ask: "What part of our deployment process allowed this broken code to get to production?"
- Instead of: "Why did you ship a bad event schema?"
- Ask: "How can we improve our schema validation and review process to catch this kind of error earlier?"
- Instead of: "You forgot to make the consumer idempotent."
- Ask: "It looks like the system re-processed some events and caused duplicates. What tools or patterns can we provide to make writing idempotent consumers the default, easy path?"

When an incident occurs, your first reaction should be curiosity, not frustration. Treat every failure as a surprise that reveals a hidden truth about your system. The goal isn't to prevent all failures—that's impossible. The goal is to learn the maximum amount from every failure so you don't make the same class of mistake twice. This mindset shift is the foundation for creating a truly resilient, self-healing organization, not just a self-healing system.

Tactic 3: Run Genuinely Blameless Post-mortems

The most powerful ritual for institutionalizing a culture of safety is the blameless post-mortem. This isn't just a meeting you hold after an outage; it's a structured, facilitated process designed to extract learnings, not assign blame. Many companies claim to do this, but they often fall into the trap of a "blameful" post-mortem in disguise, where the whole process is a subtle hunt for the "guilty" party. A true blameless post-mortem is a radical act of collective learning.

Here's how to run one effectively for an EDA-related incident:

- Set the Stage: The facilitator (who should be as neutral as possible) starts the meeting by explicitly stating the prime directive, famously articulated by Etsy's John Allspaw: "We believe that everyone involved in an incident did the best they could with the information they had at the time." This isn't about being "nice"; it's a pragmatic assumption that allows people to speak freely without fear.
- Build a Timeline, Not a Story: The first and most important task is to collaboratively build a detailed, factual timeline of events. What happened first? What happened next? What alerts fired? What commands were run? What was the state of the Google Cloud Pub/Sub subscription backlog? Who was paged? This should be a dispassionate accounting of facts, not a narrative of who did what. Use logs, metrics dashboards, and chat transcripts. The goal is to get a shared, objective understanding of the event's progression.
- Identify Contributing Factors (Plural): Significant failures are never caused by a single error. They are the result of multiple, smaller contributing factors aligning in just the right way. Your job is to uncover these systemic issues. Look for things like:
- Technical Gaps: A missing metric, ambiguous logging, a race condition in the code, a poorly configured retry mechanism.
- Process Gaps: A manual deployment step that was forgotten, a lack of a formal review for schema changes, inadequate on-call documentation.
- Knowledge Gaps: The on-call engineer wasn't familiar with this part of the system, the team didn't understand the broker's delivery guarantees.

- Focus on "How," Not "Who": The facilitator must be vigilant in steering the conversation. If someone says, "Then Bob pushed the bad schema," the facilitator should gently reframe: "Okay, so a new schema was deployed. Let's dig into the process. How does our system allow a schema change that breaks a downstream consumer to be deployed?" The focus is always on the system and the process that allowed the human to make an error.
- Generate Actionable, Owned Remediation Items: The output of the post-mortem is not a document that gets filed away. It's a list of concrete actions to improve the system's resilience. Each item must have a clear owner and a target date. These aren't punishments; they are improvements. Examples might include: "Add consumer lag monitoring for all critical event streams," "Implement a CI check that validates all schema changes against known consumers," or "Update the runbook with clear instructions for pausing a message queue."

By consistently following this process, you prove to your team that failure is not a career-limiting event, but an opportunity for collective growth.

Tactic 4: Engineer Structures for Voice

Simply telling people "please speak up" is not enough, especially in a culture that has a history of being unsafe. You have to create intentional structures and processes that actively invite and require people to contribute. You need to make silence awkward and participation easy.

One simple but effective technique is the round-robin. At key decision points in a meeting—like before finalizing a new event design—go around the room (or the Zoom call) and ask every single person for their input. No exceptions. This prevents the "loudest voices win" dynamic and gives quieter team members like Fatima a dedicated, low-pressure slot to share their thoughts. They know their turn is coming, so they can prepare their thoughts.

Another powerful tool is assigning a designated devil's advocate. For any major architectural proposal, officially assign one person the role of finding flaws in the plan. Their job is not to be negative, but to be critical and poke holes in the argument. This does two brilliant things. First, it formalizes dissent, making it part of the process rather than an act of rebellion. Second, it removes the personal risk from the person offering the critique. They aren't being difficult; they're doing their job. This can be a rotating role, giving everyone a chance to practice critical thinking and see the system from a different perspective.

Finally, create low-friction channels for feedback. This could be an anonymous "ask the architect anything" form, dedicated office hours where anyone can drop in to discuss a concern, or using pull requests not just for code, but for architecture decision records (ADRs), creating a written, asynchronous forum for debate where the best idea can win, regardless of who it came from.

Story Time

This is a story from Francisco Arismendi Büchner, Clinical Psychologist and Co-Founder of Tapuat: Humanistic Mental Health.

The nature of a company's tasks should be the major factor guiding its processes. Whether it is an online sale or the successful launch of a rocket with people inside, the dynamics of a mature (not old) company culture is that it is professional and rational on recognition, design, and implementation of processes. As processes grow in complexity, sometimes companies do not mature with them. For that reason, the provision of psychological safety is a pre-condition for the possibility of fostering an environment for professional development.

The key lies in how explicit and intentional the goal of creating a culture of psychological safety needs to be, when questioning and reporting are integrated as a daily practice.

To illustrate it, we can go to other domains where errors in technical and event driven process could literally end up in a "Post Mortem" analysis.

Chernobyl's disaster story begins on April 26, 1986, on a Reactor of the nuclear power plant in the Ukrainian SSR, near Pripyat. Known for its horrific scale, it started with a routine but very risky experiment: a planned power shutdown test to see if the reactor's still-spinning turbines could power internal operations while diesel generators powered up.

In a catastrophic procedural failure, operators shut down critical safety systems. They lost control of the reactor, causing a massive steam explosion and a nuclear meltdown. The reactor's own design flaws made the disaster worse. The resulting radiation cloud spread across Northern Europe. It killed 31 people instantly and would indirectly kill tens of thousands more. The USSR responded with secrecy and denial. The government wanted to preserve national pride and hide any flaws in Soviet engineering. This secrecy slowed the emergency response and made the disaster's effects worse. In the end, officials blamed the catastrophe solely on "human error." They focused only on the operators' mistakes, not the deeper system failures.

Three men—Viktor Bryukhanov, Nikolai Fomin, and Anatoly Dyatlov—were imprisoned for their roles.

The catastrophic meltdown was not just a technical failure. It was a crisis caused by a complete lack of psychological safety. The company's culture was sick. It silenced concerns and made a healthy workplace impossible. Truth-telling was sacrificed for party and profit. This created a deep organizational discontentment—a feeling of unease employees live with every day, where ethics and excellence were blocked by the pursuit of gain and a false sense of camaraderie.

This organizational discontentment was rooted in a workplace defined by tension, stress, and fear. The wider Soviet culture demanded absolute compliance, fostering a powerful fear of authority. The state prioritized political mandates over technical expertise. In such an environment, where people feel their security is threatened, the mind focuses entirely on survival. They have no mental space for thriving, creating, or working to their full ethical and capable potential.

The Chernobyl disaster underscored a critical failure: operators identified safety violations but were powerless to address them. This case highlights how a culture that values secrecy and punitive measures over transparency and learning is intrinsically vulnerable to systemic breakdown. Such conditions cultivate an organizational discontentment, rooted in the deprivation of fundamental psychological requirements—namely, the need for safety, significance, and a sense of belonging.

The specific dynamics that drive a culture can be identified and used as predictors. Adlerian Theory and Transactional Analysis offer effective lenses through which to observe these signs.

From a rather general perspective the USSR system provide a textbook example of a pathological organization where fundamental needs were systematically frustrated. The unsafe working environment bred fear, leading to counterproductive fight, flight, or freeze responses, preventing optimal working conditions. Workers were denied dignity and respect, confirming that their work life was deeply unsatisfactory. When the authorities blamed the accident solely on "human error", they inflicted a deep psychological loss on the workers, suggesting that the only value derived from their job was a paycheck, robbing them of their sense of contribution. The highly hierarchical decision-making process at Chernobyl was an authoritarian model where orders flowed only from above. This system encouraged vertical striving—a mode of goal-striving where individuals strive against others, viewing colleagues as "ladder rungs" to step on to reach higher power. This desire to dominate came from a lack of belonging or perceived importance. Greater power distance suffocated the horizontal effort—cooperation towards a common, collective goal—that was necessary for security.

Given the fear of retaliation, the predictable coping mechanism was avoidance behavior. Individuals who face an organization that prioritized avoiding stress, rejection, or humiliation, utilized defensive mechanisms such as hedging, qualifying, and softening their language about concerns and mistakes, ensuring that vital safety information was suppressed.

Transactional Analysis, on the other hand, reveals how the political and corporate response functioned as a destructive game, one designed to provide a psychological payoff that absolves management of guilt.

The post-mortem response, which valued punishment over learning, set up a classic "blame culture" game. The government, acting as the Parent ego state, focused on individual operators' "violations", rather than objective and systemic analysis (Adult). The jailing of the plant managers served the psychological payoff of a classic Transactional Analysis Game, such as 'Now I've Got You.' The authorities framed the disaster as a profound 'provocation,' permitting them to unleash suppressed anger and validate a core belief in the untrustworthiness of others. This pattern is further evidenced by their use of a trivial slip—the test failure—as a pretext for rage, a distinctive maneuver in such blame-shifting games

The official declaration of "human error" allowed the authorities to claim vindication and justification for their rage against the operators. This punishment, however, did not reduce mistakes; instead, it achieved the opposite, forcing problems to be suppressed until they were too big to hide. The lack of psychological safety ensured that people facing interpersonal threat would continue to use "defensive routines" that thwarted organizational learning.

Having said that, the Chernobyl disaster demonstrated that technical solutions alone were inadequate for prevention, compelling a profound cultural and operational shift in nuclear safety. In response, the industry adapted frameworks from aviation, which had long emphasized the critical role of human factors.

Thus, the primary conclusion of multiple studies, including the analysis of Chernobyl´s disaster, has been that technical improvements alone do not reduce accidents or operational errors, as these are often caused by human factors such as poor communication, deficient team interactions, and rigid hierarchies that inhibit the expression of concerns and the reporting of any issues that could threaten the status quo of the system. In response to this, the nuclear industry stablished the so-called "safety culture", adopting aviation practices such as Crew Resource Management. This methodology, known as CRM for non-aeronautical teams or Human and Organisational Performance Training (HOP), is designed to create psychologically safe environments, promote effective communication and reduce power gradients, in order to prevent fatal consequences. At the same time, the International Reporting

System (IRS) was created to break with the culture of secrecy and punishment and replace it with a mechanism for collective learning. But integrating these systems is still a challenge, as can be seen in the nuclear industry's IRS limitation, which allows only 'authorized' users to issue reports, demonstrating the difficulty of completely overcoming the culture of opacity that catalyzed the Chernobyl disaster.

Common Pitfalls

- ✕ Confusing 'Nice' with 'Safe'. Psychological safety is not about avoiding conflict or being perpetually nice. A safe team can have vigorous, passionate debates about architectural choices. The key difference is that the conflict is about the ideas, not the people. Safety means you can challenge a colleague's proposal without fearing they will resent you for it. It's about being able to be candid, which isn't always nice, but it is always respectful.
- ✕ Running a 'Blameful' Post-mortem in Disguise. You can follow all the steps, but if the underlying tone of the questions from leadership is "I need to know who is accountable for this," the team will see right through it. If a manager asks, "So, whose on-call shift was this?" it immediately poisons the well. Leaders must actively police their own language and intent to ensure the focus stays on the system.
- ✕ Ignoring the 'Brilliant Jerk'. Often, the biggest source of fear on a team is a single, high-performing individual who is dismissive, arrogant, or quick to blame others. You cannot build a safe culture around them. Their behavior, if left unchecked, will signal to everyone else that toxicity is acceptable as long as you deliver. Addressing this behavior is a non-negotiable leadership responsibility.
- ✕ Assuming Safety is a 'One and Done' Task. You don't "achieve" psychological safety and then move on. It's like a garden; it requires constant tending. A single blame-filled meeting or a sarcastic remark from a leader can undo months of work. It must be a part of your team's daily hygiene, reinforced in every meeting, every code review, and every one-on-one.

Key Takeaways

- ☞ Safety Is a Prerequisite for Complexity. You cannot succeed with a complex, distributed architecture like EDA without a team culture that allows for open, honest, and fearless communication. The technical and cultural systems are intertwined.

- ☞ Blame the System, Not the Person. This is the fundamental mindset shift. Humans make mistakes. Your job is to build systems—both technical and social—that are resilient to those mistakes. Focus on improving the process, the tooling, and the knowledge, not on correcting the person.
- ☞ Vulnerability Is a Leadership Superpower. As a leader, being the first to say "I don't know" or "I was wrong" is the most powerful way to give your team permission to be human. It replaces fear with a shared desire to learn.
- ☞ Turn Failure into Fuel. Every incident, every bug, every outage is a source of priceless data about the weaknesses in your system. A blameless post-mortem is the ritual you use to extract that data and turn it into concrete improvements, making the entire organization smarter and more resilient.

Further Reading

- 🕮 The Fearless Organization: Creating Psychological Safety in the Workplace for Learning, Innovation, and Growth by Amy C. Edmondson. This is the foundational book on the topic. If you read nothing else, read this.
- 🕮 Project Aristotle. A summary of Google's internal research project to discover the secrets of effective teams. Their number one finding? Psychological safety. You can find their findings easily on their re:Work website.
- 🕮 "Blameless PostMortems and a Just Culture" by John Allspaw. A classic and influential blog post from his time at Etsy that laid out the principles and rationale for the blameless post-mortem process.
- 🕮 Turn the Ship Around!: A True Story of Turning Followers into Leaders by L. David Marquet. While not directly about psychological safety, this book is a masterclass in pushing control and decision-making down to the people with the information, which is a key outcome of a safe environment.

Strategy 22

Leading Continuous Evolution

You did it. The big push is over. You fought the good fight, you convinced the skeptics, and you shipped the first wave of services on your new Event-Driven Architecture (EDA). The teams are buzzing. Features that used to take months are now shipping in weeks. The system feels more resilient, more responsive. You even got that congratulatory email from the CTO you've been waiting for. For a moment, you can breathe. The project is a success.

But a few quarters later, a strange feeling starts to creep in. The buzz has faded. You hear whispers of a team building a new service that completely ignores the event standards you worked so hard to establish. Another team complains that the central schema registry is becoming a bottleneck, so they've started embedding schemas directly in their messages again—the exact problem you set out to solve. The "new way" is starting to feel a little… old. The clean, loosely-coupled architecture you designed is slowly, almost imperceptibly, starting to fray at the edges. The momentum is gone, and you're worried the whole thing is heading back toward the same tangled mess you just escaped.

You are here if...

- The initial victory of launching your EDA has given way to the quiet, grinding reality of maintaining it.

- You see teams drifting away from established patterns, if innovation has stalled, and if your once-gleaming architecture is starting to gather dust.
- You've won the battle, but you're starting to realize that the war for architectural sanity is never really over.
- You're facing the challenge of keeping the momentum alive for the long haul.

The core principle here is simple but profound: An Event-Driven Architecture is not a project you finish; it's a living system you cultivate. Think of yourself less as a builder who constructs a building and walks away, and more as a gardener. You've planted the seeds and helped them sprout, but now you must tend to the garden. You have to water it, pull the weeds, prune the branches, and enrich the soil. If you walk away, the garden will inevitably be reclaimed by nature—in our world, that means complexity, entropy, and chaos. The goal isn't to achieve a final, perfect state but to create a system and a culture that can adapt, learn, and improve continuously. This shift in mindset, from "project" to "process," is the key to long-term success with EDA.

The Action Plan

To cultivate your EDA garden, you need more than just good intentions. You need a set of deliberate, repeatable practices that create a self-reinforcing cycle of improvement. This isn't about adding heavy bureaucracy; it's about building lightweight structures that make continuous evolution the path of least resistance.

Tactic 1: Build the Feedback Engine

You can't fix problems you don't know about. The first and most critical step is to build robust, multi-channel feedback loops that tell you what's working, what's broken, and where the next headache is coming from. Don't wait for developers to get so fed up they start working around your system; go out and actively solicit their feedback.

A great way to do this is by establishing an Architecture Guild or a Community of Practice (CoP) focused on EDA. This is not another top-down review board. It's a grassroots forum for engineers from different teams to meet regularly—maybe every two weeks or once a month—and just talk. What cool things have they built? What annoying problems have they run into? Which event pattern turned out to be a total nightmare in production? These sessions are your primary sensor network. They surface the real, on-the-ground challenges and successes, creating a shared understanding and a sense of collective ownership.

Next, formalize how good ideas get turned into standards. A lightweight Request for Comments (RFC) process is perfect for this. When a developer in the CoP proposes a new way to handle event versioning, don't let it just be a conversation. Encourage them to write it up in a simple, one-page document. The RFC doesn't have to be a novel; it just needs to state the problem, the proposed solution, and the trade-offs. You then share it in a public place (like a Git repo or a wiki) and invite comments. This process is amazing because it's inclusive, it's transparent, and it creates a written history of your architectural decisions. It turns "one person's clever idea" into "our team's agreed-upon best practice."

Finally, get data from your tools. If you've built a CLI to help developers create new services or publish schemas, add some basic telemetry. You don't need to spy on them, but understanding which commands are used most, which ones fail often, or how long a certain step takes can give you priceless, unbiased insights into where the real friction is in your developer experience. This quantitative data, combined with the qualitative feedback from the CoP, gives you a 360-degree view of your architecture's health.

Tactic 2: Schedule the Pruning

Good intentions aren't enough. If you don't make time to review and adapt your architecture, it will never happen. You need to put it on the calendar. The act of scheduling these reviews signals to the entire organization that architectural evolution is a priority, not an afterthought.

Start with Quarterly Architecture Reviews. This is a dedicated session with key stakeholders—lead engineers, product managers, maybe even a friendly director—to look at the EDA from a higher level. The questions here aren't about code, but about outcomes. Are we still delivering features faster? Has our system availability improved? Is the business able to launch new initiatives that weren't possible before? You should also review the key metrics from your feedback engine. Are we seeing more "rogue" events without proper schemas? Is the time it takes for a new developer to get their first service running getting longer? This meeting is your chance to zoom out and ensure the garden is still producing the fruit the business actually wants.

Just as important as adding new things is removing old ones. Your architecture will inevitably accumulate cruft: outdated event schemas, deprecated services, and patterns that seemed like a good idea at the time. This is architectural rot, and it makes the system harder to understand and work with. To fight this, create formal Sunsetting Rituals. When a new version of an event is introduced, the old one should have a clear expiration date. When a service is retired, there should be a checklist to make sure it's fully removed from the ecosystem, not just left to linger as a zombie process. Celebrating the removal of old code and complexity can be just as powerful as celebrating the launch of a new feature. It shows the team you value simplicity and maintainability.

Tactic 3: Scan the Horizon

Your organization doesn't exist in a vacuum. The world of event-driven systems is constantly evolving. New technologies, new protocols, and new patterns emerge all the time. If you only look inward, you risk your architecture becoming a technological dead end. You need to build a bridge to the outside world.

Formally encourage your senior engineers to dedicate time to "scouting." This could be a few hours every Friday afternoon or a dedicated "innovation day" once a quarter. Their job is to look beyond your company's immediate problems and explore what's happening in the broader ecosystem. What's new with projects like CloudEvents? Are there new patterns for handling long-running processes that could solve a problem you're having? How are other companies using tools like RabbitMQ or Google Cloud Pub/Sub in interesting ways? They should bring these findings back to the Architecture Guild to spark discussion and inspire new experiments.

A great way to structure this exploration is by creating and maintaining an EDA Tech Radar, inspired by the ThoughtWorks original. This is a simple, visual way to categorize different technologies, patterns, and tools based on your organization's opinion. You can have four rings: Adopt (things you should be using), Trial (things you should be experimenting with), Assess (things you should be looking into), and Hold (things you should avoid). This isn't a top-down decree; it's a living document created collaboratively by the CoP. It serves as a guide for teams, helping them make smart choices without having to re-evaluate every single option from scratch.

Finally, encourage and fund external engagement. Send your engineers to conferences like the AsyncAPI Conference, API Days, GOTO, and others. Give them the budget to buy books. Support them if they want to contribute to an open-source project that you rely on. The insights, connections, and motivation they bring back are worth far more than the cost of a plane ticket. When your team is part of the global conversation, they bring the world's best ideas back home.

Tactic 4: Cultivate the Culture of Tinkering

Ultimately, continuous evolution is about people. You can have the best processes and tools in the world, but if your culture punishes failure and discourages experimentation, you'll stagnate. You need to create an environment where people feel safe to try new things, even if they don't work out.

One of the most powerful things you can do is celebrate "smart" failures. When a team tries a new event sourcing pattern and it doesn't scale as they expected, don't let them bury it. Instead, invite them to the CoP to present a post-mortem. What was the hypothesis? What did they build? What happened? What did they learn? By treating this as a valuable learning experience for the entire organization, you send a clear message: we value learning more than we fear failure. This removes the fear that holds back so much innovation.

You can also supercharge this by organizing internal "EDA Days" or hackathons. Give everyone a day or two to just play. They can work on a nagging problem with the developer tooling, experiment with a new broker feature, or try to build a wild proof-of-concept that connects two disparate systems in a new way. The goal isn't necessarily to produce a production-ready feature, but to generate ideas, build skills, and create a burst of creative energy. It's like tilling the soil in your garden—it loosens things up and prepares the ground for new growth.

Finally, identify and empower your champions. In every organization, there are individuals who are naturally passionate about this stuff. They are the ones who are already experimenting on their own time, answering questions in Slack, and advocating for better practices. Find these people. Give them a platform in the CoP. Acknowledge their contributions publicly. Make them formal mentors for new hires. These champions become your distributed leadership team, scaling the culture of continuous evolution across the entire organization far more effectively than any central committee ever could.

Common Pitfalls

- ✕ Avoid: The "Governance" Trap. It's really easy for your well-intentioned Architecture Guild and RFC process to bloat into a slow, bureaucratic "Architecture Review Board." If getting a simple change approved takes six weeks and three meetings, developers will just work around you. Keep it lightweight. The goal is guardrails that make it easy to do the right thing, not gates that stop progress. An RFC process should take days, not months.
- ✕ Avoid: Forgetting the "Why." As you get deep into the technical weeds of event versioning or broker configurations, it's easy to lose sight of the business reason you're doing this. Never let a technical discussion end without asking, "How does this proposed change help us deliver value to customers faster, reduce risk, or lower costs?" Tying every architectural decision, no matter how small, back to a business outcome keeps you honest and makes it much easier to justify your work to leadership.

- × Avoid: "Project-itis." Don't save up all your desired changes for a big, monolithic "EDA 2.0" project. That approach is slow, risky, and creates a huge blast radius. Instead, embrace a continuous stream of small, incremental improvements. Upgrading a client library, rolling out a new event pattern, sunsetting an old service—these should be small, routine tasks, not massive, scary projects. The goal is evolution, not revolution.

Key Takeaways

- ☞ EDA is a Garden, Not a Building. This is the core mindset shift. Stop thinking about your EDA as a project that you "finish." It's a living system that requires constant care, attention, and cultivation. Your job is to be the head gardener, not the architect of a finished monument.
- ☞ Make Feedback Your Oxygen. You cannot guide what you cannot see. Proactively build systems to listen to your developers and your platform. A Community of Practice, a lightweight RFC process, and tooling telemetry are not "nice-to-haves"; they are your essential sensory organs for architectural health.
- ☞ Put Evolution on the Calendar. Good intentions are not a strategy. If you don't schedule time for review, pruning, and adaptation, it will get pushed aside by the tyranny of the urgent. Quarterly reviews and formal sunsetting processes make evolution an intentional, respected part of your engineering rhythm.
- ☞ Connect to the Outside World. Your best ideas won't always come from inside your own walls. Encourage your team to scan the horizon for new technologies and patterns. A Tech Radar and active participation in the wider tech community prevent your architecture from becoming obsolete and keep your team's skills sharp.

Further Reading

- 🕮 Building Evolutionary Architectures by Neal Ford, Rebecca Parsons, and Patrick Kua. This is the foundational text on this topic. It provides the theory and vocabulary for creating architectures that are designed to change over time.
- 🕮 Cultivating Communities of Practice by Etienne Wenger, Richard McDermott, and William M. Snyder. If you want to get serious about setting up your Architecture Guild or CoP, this book is the definitive guide. It covers the practical steps for launching and sustaining these powerful groups.

- 📖 The ThoughtWorks Technology Radar. Visit the ThoughtWorks website and explore their public Tech Radars. It's the best example of the "Scan the Horizon" tactic in action and a great source of inspiration for creating your own.

Conclusion

Your Enduring Role as an EDA Catalyst

We're at the end of the book, but we're at the very beginning of your real journey. If you've read this far, thank you. You've invested your time, and my goal has been to give you a playbook that respects that investment—one packed with real-world strategies, not just high-level theory. You've seen the scenarios, wrestled with the challenges, and absorbed the action plans. You now have a set of tools designed for one of the hardest jobs in technology: driving foundational change inside an organization.

But let's be crystal clear about one thing. This book was never really about Event-Driven Architecture.

EDA is the context, the "what." It's the technical solution that promises a future of more resilient, scalable, and loosely-coupled systems. It's a fantastic solution for a whole class of modern business problems. But the principles in this playbook—the strategies for understanding resistance, for speaking the language of the business, for building momentum, and for navigating politics—are about the "how." And in any significant organizational change, the "how" is always, always harder than the "what."

You picked up this book because you want to build better systems. You're finishing it, I hope, equipped to build something far more important: consensus, momentum, and lasting change.

The Playbook as a Living Guide

Think of this book not as a rigid instruction manual but as a set of recipes from a professional kitchen. A good chef doesn't just blindly follow a recipe card; they understand the core principles behind it. They know when to add a bit more salt because their ingredients are different. They know how to substitute one component for another based on what's fresh and available. They adapt.

You must do the same. The strategies in this playbook are your ingredients and techniques. Your organization—with its unique history, culture, budget cycles, and personalities—is your kitchen. You are the chef.

Context is Everything

A strategy that works wonders in a fast-moving startup will fall completely flat in a 150-year-old financial institution. The approach for Alex's retail company, which might prioritize speed, would get Lola shut down before she even started at her bank. She needs to lean heavily on strategies like Securing Leadership Backing and Discovering Strategic Value just to get a hearing.

Before you apply any strategy from this book, take a hard look around you.

- What is your company's tolerance for risk? Are you encouraged to experiment, or is every failure a mark against you?
- How are decisions really made? Is it in the official meeting, or in the 15-minute chat that happens before the meeting?
- What does your leadership actually care about this quarter? Is it top-line growth, operational efficiency, or breaking into a new market?

Your ability to read the room—and the entire organization—is more important than your ability to design the perfect event-driven system. The strategies in this book are your toolkit. Your context determines which tool you pull out.

Combine and Create

The strategies aren't meant to be used in isolation. They are designed to be layered on top of each other. You don't just choose one. You might start with Strategy 2: Mapping the Stakeholder Landscape to understand who holds influence. Based on that map, you might realize you need to focus on Strategy 5: Addressing Developer Concerns for a key team, while simultaneously working with business leaders on Strategy 7: Selecting the Strategic Pilot to prove immediate value.

Advocacy is a creative act. You'll find yourself blending these ideas, adapting the language, and inventing your own tactics based on the core principles. That's not just okay; it's the whole point. The goal isn't to perfectly execute "The Shift Playbook." The goal is to make the shift happen in your organization.

Technology Changes, People Don't

In five years, we might be talking about a hot new message broker that makes Kafka or Pulsar look ancient. There will be new patterns, new protocols, and new buzzwords. The technical landscape of EDA will absolutely evolve.

But the human challenges are timeless.

You will always have to secure funding from leaders who don't understand the tech. You will always have to persuade overworked engineers to learn a new way of doing things. You will always have to deal with skeptics, build alliances, and demonstrate value. The core principles of influence, communication, and strategic thinking will be just as relevant then as they are today. That's what this playbook is really about. It's a guide to the human systems that sit on top of our technical ones.

Final Thoughts on Leading Transformative Change

If you only take one thing away from this entire book, let it be this: your success as an EDA advocate has less to do with your architectural diagrams and more to do with your ability to lead people through uncertainty. Your job title might be "Principal Engineer" or "Solutions Architect," but your effective role is "Change Agent."

This requires you to be more than just a technologist. It requires you to be a translator, a diplomat, a coach, and a strategist. It's a huge ask, and it's not for everyone. But if you're ready for the challenge, you need to cultivate a few key qualities. These aren't "soft skills"; they are the essential toolkit for a modern technical leader.

- Unrelenting Patience. This is a marathon, not a sprint. You will propose an idea and hear "no." You will hear "no" five more times. You will finally get a "maybe," only to have the budget reallocated. You will explain the difference between a message and an event for the hundredth time. Change at the architectural level happens on a scale of quarters and years, not days and weeks. Patience isn't passive waiting; it's active persistence.
- Deep Empathy. The engineer who pushes back on your new standard isn't being difficult; they're afraid of a new tool slowing them down when they're

already behind on their sprint goals. The manager who denies your budget request isn't clueless; they're under immense pressure to hit a quarterly revenue target, and your project sounds like a costly distraction. Resistance is just a signal of an unmet need or an unaddressed fear. Your job is not to crush resistance but to understand it. Empathy is your primary diagnostic tool.

- Strategic Communication. Being the smartest person in the room is useless if you can't make your ideas understood and compelling to everyone else. You have to learn to switch your language constantly. With your engineering peers, you can debate the merits of at-least-once vs. exactly-once delivery. With a product manager, you talk about shipping features faster and with fewer bugs. With a CFO, you talk about reducing operational costs and lowering the risk of catastrophic outages. You must become a master translator, converting technical benefits into business value.
- Rock-Solid Resilience. You will fail. A project will get canceled. A key ally will leave the company. You'll get negative feedback. It's going to happen. The defining quality of successful change agents is not that they never get knocked down, but that they always get back up. They treat setbacks as learning opportunities, not as referendums on their abilities. Resilience is the engine that keeps you going when patience wears thin.

This is the work. It's messy, it's frustrating, and it's often invisible. You won't get a promotion for "demonstrating resilience" or a bonus for "showing empathy." But these are the things that actually make the difference. These are the skills that allow great technology to actually see the light of day.

The Road Ahead

You're standing at a trailhead. You have the map, the compass, and a good understanding of the terrain. The temptation can be to plan the entire multi-year expedition before taking the first step. Don't.

Start small.

Find one team. One business problem. One event. Use Strategy 7: Selecting the Strategic Pilot. Get a small, undeniable win. Use that success story to build momentum for the next step, leveraging Strategy 9: Broadcasting Early Successes. Let your EDA adoption grow organically, pulled by proven value, not pushed by a grand, top-down mandate. A quiet, successful proof-of-concept is infinitely more powerful than the most beautiful presentation a C-suite executive has ever seen.

You are not alone on this journey. All over the world, in companies of every size, there are other architects and engineers just like you, trying to make this same shift happen. They are facing the same skeptical managers, the same resistant teams, and the same organizational inertia. Connect with them. Find them in communities like the AsyncAPI community, in forums, and at conferences. Share your war stories, learn from their successes, and remember that this is a shared struggle. And on a personal note, my door is always open. I genuinely love hearing about a tricky problem or a hard-won success story, so don't hesitate to reach out. This isn't a pitch for consulting; it's an open invitation to connect with someone else who is passionate about this stuff.

The shift to an event-driven world is happening, with or without you. The question is whether it will happen to your organization—chaotically and reactively—or whether it will happen for your organization, guided by a thoughtful, strategic, and human-centered approach.

You have the playbook. You understand the principles. You are the catalyst.

Now, go lead the shift.

Resources & Tools

Stay Current with the Latest EDA Assets

The world of event-driven architecture and engineering strategy moves fast. To ensure you always have access to the most up-to-date templates, checklists, and technical deep-dives mentioned in this book, I maintain a live Digital Resource Library.

Access the library here: https://leadtheshift.co

Acknowledgements

People think writing a book is a solo job. They're wrong. I did the typing alone, but the ideas here come from a thousand conversations and shared struggles. This book wasn't built in some boring boardroom. It was built in public—messy and iterative, just like the software we love.

To the eight incredible storytellers who shared their wisdom: David Roldán, David Pardo, Emmanuel Paraskakis, Francisco Arismendi, Jonas Lagoni, and Samir Amzani. Thank you for trusting me with your stories. You brought perspectives that go way beyond code, covering everything from psychology to investment. You proved that leadership challenges are universal. This book would be a hollow shell without your insights.

To my "Notion Squad"—the 40+ beta readers who jumped into the chaos while the cement was still wet. Thank you for putting up with my typos and my half-baked thoughts. You didn't just read a book; you helped debug it. Your feedback was the unit test this project really needed.

To the AsyncAPI community. This playbook was forged in our Slack channels and GitHub issues. You taught me that being right about the tech isn't enough. To actually change things, you have to win hearts before you can merge Pull Requests. Thank you for being the best testing ground an architect could ask for.

And finally, to you, the reader. Whether you are a Software Engineer shipping your first feature or a CTO setting the vision, thank you for trusting me with your time.

Now, go build something great.

— Fran

www.ingramcontent.com/pod-product-compliance
Lightning Source LLC
Chambersburg PA
CBHW050525240926
51846CB00003B/702
* 9 7 8 8 4 0 9 7 6 1 5 2 4 *